KU-413-098

CONTENTS
The Pictures

PRECIOUS MOMENTS FROM THE FAMILY ALBUM TO
PROVIDE YOU WITH COMFORT IN THE LONG YEARS TO
COME was first performed on 25th July 1967 at the
Manchester University Theatre, when it was directed by
the Author, with the following cast:

FATHER	George Taylor
MOTHER	Helen Prime
SON	Richard Martin
DAUGHTER	Clare Venables
GRANDMOTHER	Maggie Mash

The play received its first professional performance at
the Mercury Theatre, London, on 11th December, 1967,
when it was directed by the Author, with the following cast:

FATHER	Heinz Bernard
MOTHER	Mary Henry
SON	Jack Chissick
DAUGHTER	Judy Liebert
GRANDMOTHER	Peggy Bullock

The Author would like to thank Clare Venables, Richard
Martin, Susan Chew, and, especially, Gary Kahn for all
their suggestions and advice.

PLAYSCRIPT 24

'precious moments from the family album to provide you with comfort in the long years to come'

naftali yavin

CALDER AND BOYARS · LONDON

First published in Great Britain 1969
by Calder and Boyars Limited
18 Brewer Street London W1R 4AS

© Naftali Yavin 1969

All performing rights in this play
are strictly reserved and applications
for performance should be made to
Lom Associates Limited
6a Maddox Street London W1

No performance of the play
may be given unless a licence
has been obtained prior to rehearsal

ALL RIGHTS RESERVED

SBN 7145 0635 4 Cloth edition
SBN 7145 0636 2 Paper

Printed in Great Britain
by The Pitman Press
Bath, Somerset

QUEEN MARGARET COLLEGE LIBRARY

4/11/69
32704

PRECIOUS MOMENTS FROM THE FAMILY ALBUM TO PROVIDE YOU WITH COMFORT IN THE LONG YEARS TO COME

The six pictures in this very amusing and penetrating play are six separate scenes in the life of one family, to be performed in any order or with any combination of two or more scenes. Cocking snooks at the frail structure on which matriarchal society is built, at Freudian analysis and at collectors' mania, it also examines with great insight and seriousness the way in which each member of the family will fight to maintain what he or she considers his position within the unit, the effect of different parental attitudes, from indifference to misplaced understanding, on their bewildered children and the binding force which can cut a family off from the outside world. At the same time the play lays bare the much wider existential, moral and sociological problems underlying the relations of the individual with his world.

Five characters, representing three generations, each make equally valid contributions to the stimulating, humourous and fast-moving action of the play, speaking turn by turn in monosyllabic abuse, in childish endearments, in the desperate incoherence of the frustrated desire to communicate and the daily hyperbole of unthinking familiarity. Though each picture has a definite style of its own, together they make a striking whole.

Naftali Yavin was born in Haifa, Israel in 1936. He trained at the Habimah National Drama School and read philosophy at the University of Tel Aviv. His first full-length play won the Israeli Arts Council award in 1965 and a year later the British Council awarded him a bursary in order to obtain a post-graduate diploma in Drama at Manchester University. He now works as a director with The Other Company, and has directed plays for them at the Ambience and the Institute of Contemporary Arts.

QUEEN MARGARET COLLEGE

100 094 494

To Your Family

PRECIOUS MOMENTS
FROM THE FAMILY ALBUM
TO PROVIDE YOU WITH COMFORT
IN THE LONG YEARS TO COME

CHARACTERS

FATHER

MOTHER

SON

DAUGHTER

GRANDMOTHER

A MAN

A WOMAN

MOTHER'S DAY

Characters
FATHER
MOTHER
SON
DAUGHTER
GRANDMOTHER

(The bedroom. A dressing table, mirror, cupboards.
Only the conventional double bed is missing. In different
places vases with flowers.
DAUGHTER is arranging the flowers. SON is standing
on a ladder hanging a banner saying 'All our sincere
and best wishes from the bottom of our hearts'. In
another corner is a sign saying 'We love Mummy'.)

SON. (Very cheerfully to DAUGHTER) Yoohoo!

DAUGHTER. (To SON, also very cheerfully) Yoohooyoo-
hoohoohoo.

(They begin to sing the first bars of a very sweet
melody; then they burst into laughter.)

SON. Come and give me a hand, sweetie-pie.

DAUGHTER. Coming honeybunch. (She goes over to him.
Helps him hang the banner.) Ohoooooeeeee it's so
lovely.

(SON laughs with satisfaction)

Oh yes, oh yes, pretty, sweetie, tweety-tweety.

(They laugh joyfully. DAUGHTER returns to the flowers.
Enter GRANDMOTHER. She brings with her some old
family photographs, puts them in various places in the
room, while talking to herself.)

GRANDMOTHER. Oh bless the Lord, bless the Lord.

SON. (With great affection to GRANDMOTHER) Granny-loo,
Granny-poo.

GRANDMOTHER. Bless the Lord.

SON. (To GRANDMOTHER) Tottsie Wootsie Pootsie.

DAUGHTER. (Smells flowers) Aaaaaaaaah... (She finishes
arranging the flowers, looks around with great satisfaction.) Oh, it's so beautiful, simply and utterly
beautiful! (She starts singing again.)

SON. Oh my, oh my, oh my...

GRANDMOTHER. Bless the Lord.

(SON and DAUGHTER look at her sympathetically, laugh
and start singing together.

Enter FATHER, his hands full of parcels, nicely wrapped.
They turn to him, he puts the parcels down and looks
around.)

FATHER. (With great satisfaction) Oho, oho, oho!

(They all look at each other, very self-satisfied.)

Shhhh... (He takes out an atomizer and sprays the room.)

ALL. (Breathe deeply) Aaaaaaah...

FATHER. And now?

SON. And now?

DAUGHTER. And now...

12

FATHER. (Short pause. Tension.) THE BED!

SON. (Enthusiastically) It's here?

FATHER. Here.

DAUGHTER. (Quickly) Quickly-quickly-quickly-quickly.

(They all rush out except GRANDMOTHER. She sits on a chair, sighs deeply out of sheer enjoyment.)

GRANDMOTHER. Bless the Lord.

(SON re-appears, his back to the audience, carrying one end of the bed.)

FATHER. (Off.) Careful now.

(They bring in the bed, put it in its place then stand around it, and look at it with great satisfaction.)

DAUGHTER. Woweeeee!

(SON makes a long kissing sound.)

GRANDMOTHER. Oh, blast our almighty Lord!

(FATHER laughs smugly, caresses the bedstead, and makes sounds of enjoyment.

The children look at him, then at one another, and giggle.

FATHER looks at them and giggles. Short pause.

GRANDMOTHER goes to the bed, and moves her hand over it.)

GRANDMOTHER. (With a burst of what might be called long forgotten lust) Grrrrr...

(All giggle then jump on the bed laughing and shouting - 'Crash! Bash! Boom!' etc. They keep it going for quite a while until FATHER says)

13

FATHER. Enough - nough - nough. (Clasps his hands.)
Come on, now, children, come on... enough is enough.

(They relax, then get off the bed and bring sheets etc.
from the cupboard, put them on the bed and stand
around and look at it. FATHER looks around, and rubs
his hands with great satisfaction.)

That's it, everything is ready now.

ALL. Everything.

DAUGHTER. (Impatiently) Shall we bring her in now?

FATHER. (Gives a last glance round) Everyone ready?

(All nod their heads and go to their places. Children
near the door, FATHER in the centre. He counts with
increasing speed.)

Seven, six, five, three, one, boom!!

(The children open the door. MOTHER is seen. She is
blindfold. All sing 'For she's a jolly good fellow'. The
children go to her, and bring her to the bed, then return
to both sides of the room. Now FATHER goes to her
and takes the blindfold off. All burst into cheers)

MOTHER. (Tears of happiness choking her) I... I...
I'm so... so... (She bursts into tears, FATHER hands
her a handkerchief, and she blows her nose.) I never...
imagined... it's... it's... (She cannot speak, out of
sheer happiness.)

ALL. (Shouting, whistling, clapping etc.) Yipee! Horray!
(All go over to MOTHER)

FATHER. Many happy returns of the day.

SON. Many happy returns of the year.

GRANDMOTHER. Many happy returns from God.

DAUGHTER. Many happy returns my foot.

14

FATHER. (Quietens them) Sh...h...h...h... (They hush.
In a pompous tone) Our beloved dearest and most
sweetest Mummy, with the utmost gratitude for all
the things you have done for us all these precious years.

ALL. (Repeating after him, same tone) Our beloved,
dearest and sweetest Mummy etc.

MOTHER. It's really... too... much...

FATHER. You deserve it! You deserve much more! We'll
never be able to pay you back all we owe you.

CHILDREN. (In chorus) Never! Never!

GRANDMOTHER. Bless the Lord! Bless the Lord!

MOTHER. I... you're all so... (She is so excited, she
can't find the words.) You're all... you are...
(She almost faints.)

ALL. Poochy moochy choochy foochy woochy...

MOTHER. (With tremendous enjoyment) Ohhhhhhhhhhhh.

ALL. (Making baby cooing noises) A - boobooboobooboooo.

FATHER. Shhh. Let Mother speak.

MOTHER. (Slowly, with great effort) All my life, all my
life I've been waiting for this day. (They all look at
each other and giggle.) Now I know my life has not
been wasted. (They push one another and exchange
glances which express something like 'What did I tell
you'.) I never asked anything from you.

ALL. Right. Right.

MOTHER. I never wanted you to give me presents, nice
dresses, furs, jewellery, gold, diamonds.

ALL. (Approving but aggressive) Right. Right.

MOTHER. All I wanted was to know that you love me.

ALL. (To each other, pleased) Aha! Aha!

MOTHER. With all your heart.

ALL. Oho! Oho!

MOTHER. And all your soul.

ALL. Gee-up! Gee-up!

MOTHER. And all your eyes.

FATHER. (Joining in) And all your hands and chests!

SON, MOTHER & FATHER. And bellies.

DAUGHTER, SON, MOTHER & FATHER. And bottoms.

GRANDMOTHER. (On her own) And kidneys, intestines, entrails and guts!

ALL. Gee-up! Gee-up! Gee-up!

    (Pause)

MOTHER. But I don't deserve all this.

ALL. Oh no!

MOTHER. Yes, yes, I wasn't a good wife to my husband.

FATHER. Oh no.

MOTHER. I didn't have enough respect for my Mother.

GRANDMOTHER. Hail the Lord.

MOTHER. I didn't understand my own children.

SON & DAUGHTER. (Plucking their lips baby-fashion) Blabablaba.

    (MOTHER cries. ALL cry.)

MOTHER. (Recovering) But today, today, at last I know, I really know that you really, honestly, truly (Slowly) lo-ve me.

ALL. (Quickly) Love, love, love.

(She laughs happily. ALL laugh happily. A pause)

MOTHER. Do you know what we are going to do today?

ALL. (Enthusiastically) What, what?

MOTHER. We are going to do whatever you want to do.

FATHER. Oh, no, we'll do whatever you want to do.

MOTHER. No, no my darlings, whatever you want.

DAUGHTER & SON. (Aggressively) What you want.

MOTHER. (Aggressively) You!

ALL. (Aggressively) You! You!

(Short pause)

MOTHER. All right, what do I want?

ALL. What?

MOTHER. What you want.

ALL. Really? Really?

MOTHER. And what do you want?

ALL. What? What?

MOTHER. What I want.

ALL. Really? Really?

MOTHER. I know you.

ALL. You don't say.

MOTHER. Better than you know yourselves.

ALL. Sure! Sure!

MOTHER. (Triumphantly) Mother is everything in life, isn't she?

ALL. Sure, sure!

MOTHER. So?

ALL. So?

MOTHER. First of all - the presents.

ALL. The presents, the presents.

> (They all run and get the parcels. Then they walk around singing a harvest hymn. They put the parcels down against the bed. In chorus)

> We bring you the very first of our harvest, the best of our crops, the best of our flesh and blood, our hearts, and souls.

> (They stop. A pause. They look at each other, nudge each other. At last GRANDMOTHER steps forward, hands her present to MOTHER. MOTHER opens it. It is a pram.

GRANDMOTHER. Charming, isn't it?

> (The CHILDREN giggle.)

MOTHER. Hush, little devils. (To GRANDMOTHER) Oh dear me, you'll be the death of me.

GRANDMOTHER. (Gets into pram) Remember?

MOTHER. (Melting with pleasure) Ohhh!

> (GRANDMOTHER bawls like a baby.)

MOTHER. (To GRANDMOTHER) Say Mummy.

GRANDMOTHER. (With great difficulty, syllable by syllable) Mmmmm... Da...dddy...

MOTHER. Say Mummy.

GRANDMOTHER. (As before) Mmmm... Da...ddy...

MOTHER. (Getting aggressive) Say Mummy. Mummy.

GRANDMOTHER. (Crying) Daddy.

MOTHER. (Screaming) Mummy.

GRANDMOTHER. (Shouting) Daddy.

ALL. (With MOTHER) Mummy. Mummy. Mummy.

GRANDMOTHER. (With great effort) Mmmmmmm... Mmmmmmu...my.

MOTHER. (Victoriously) She said Mummy.

GRANDMOTHER. Mmmmmmm. Mmmmmmmu...my.

MOTHER. She's saying Mummy.

GRANDMOTHER. (With her last strength) Mmmuu...my. (She freezes, and sits motionless in the pram, her eyes wide open, without any expression.)

MOTHER. That's enough. Let Granny rest now. She must be very tired. (Short pause) It's about time, actually. (Short pause.) She's so old.

(SON and DAUGHTER approach GRANDMOTHER)

SON. (As if reciting) 'Grandmother, what big eyes you have.'

DAUGHTER. (Like SON) Grandmother, what a big mouth you have.'

SON. (To MOTHER) She doesn't answer.

MOTHER. (Sad) She's so old... (Pause. She is sad. To FATHER, complaining) Why don't you do something to please me?

FATHER. (Neighing) Neigh...

MOTHER. (Refusing) Grrrr...

FATHER. (Hopping round) Neigh...

SON & DAUGHTER. (Imitating him) Neigh...

MOTHER. Boo, boo, you are dirty little animals.

(They stop. Enthusiastically to FATHER)

Oh, I know! Do some of those exercises that you used to do so beautifully for me just after we got married. (Nostalgically) Oh, it was love at first sight. You were so charming, so elegant, so well-dressed, stiff collar hat and cane... you looked so continental... Don't you remember your exercises?

FATHER. Me????

MOTHER. Yes, you!

FATHER. (Surprised) What kind of exercises did I do?

MOTHER. Oh, all sorts - to keep fit, to lose weight, to strengthen your muscles, all sorts.

FATHER. I don't remember.

MOTHER. Do one now. Just a tiny, weeny bit of one.

FATHER. But I...

MOTHER. You don't want to be nice to me!

FATHER. But... I... can't... any more...

MOTHER. You certainly can: if you really wanted to, you could. Just one, one for me.

SON & DAUGHTER. Please do, Daddy, please do.

FATHER. (Aside to MOTHER) But the children.

MOTHER. Nonsense, they're grown up now.

FATHER. I really can't.

MOTHER. You see, that's how you treat me, that's the sort of husband you are. A fine example to your children. Good Father you make.

SON & DAUGHTER. Boo, Daddy. Booo...

FATHER. I... (With effort) Maybe I do remember one.

SON & DAUGHTER. Oh! Oh! Daddy is going to do some exercises for us! Hurrah for Daddy! Hurrah!

MOTHER. That's my man! That's my hero! I'll give you the beat.

FATHER. But...

MOTHER. (In time to the beat) One, two. One two.

(FATHER starts to do the exercise slowly. MOTHER quickens the beat. He tries to catch up)

One, two. One two.

(He gets tired and reduces speed.)

Once more - one two. One two. One two.

SON & DAUGHTER. (In time) Once more! Once more!

MOTHER. Faster! Faster! Once more! One, two! One two! Again, again! More, more! (Her breathing gets heavier and heavier. FATHER getting slower and slower. At last he falls down. Gradually MOTHER returns to normal breathing.) My wonderful man, my sweet hero.

SON & DAUGHTER. (Casually) He fell.

MOTHER. Oh yes, he's not the man he used to be.

SON. What's wrong with him?

MOTHER. He shouldn't have tried so hard. The party was too much for him. Put him in a chair.

(The CHILDREN put him in a chair. He sits without expression, his head turned towards MOTHER.)

DAUGHTER. (To MOTHER) Like Granny.

SON. (Goes over to GRANDMOTHER) Oh Grandmother, what big...

MOTHER. Hush, children. Let her rest in peace.

(SON and DAUGHTER turn to FATHER)

SON & DAUGHTER. (To FATHER) Tally-ho! Tally-ho! Make the fox come out of his hole!

MOTHER. Hush, children.

SON & DAUGHTER. (Hopping around, blowing horns, barking etc. imitating a fox hunt.) Yoohoo! Toot-toot! Toot-tooot! Bow-wow-wow...

MOTHER. Children!

SON & DAUGHTER. (As if reciting) Foxy, foxy, out you come! Foxy, foxy here we are. (They burst out laughing)

MOTHER. Hush, children; let Daddy rest. Come now, come to Mummy. Mummy will tell you a story. You'd like Mummy to tell you a nice story, wouldn't you?

SON & DAUGHTER. (Running to her, plucking their lips, baby-fashion) Blabablaba.

MOTHER. Sit here my loves.

(They sit)

MOTHER. Do you want Mummy to tell you how you were born?

SON & DAUGHTER. (Together, reciting) Tally-ho! Tally-ho! Make the fox...

MOTHER. Hush now, hush.

(They stop)

Listen now.

(They get ready to listen)

That's better. Well now, once upon a time, Mummy had a big, big belly...

SON. Why?

MOTHER. Ssshhhh! And the belly became bigger and bigger, blowing up and up, until it became the biggest belly in the whole world. And Mummy was so happy, she loved her big and wonderful belly so much...

SON. Like Auntie Nelly's belly?

MOTHER. Oh no! It was a much, much bigger belly. But one day the belly disappeared, and Mummy was so sad. She loved her sweet belly so much. Now Mummy was empty, without her belly, like a deflated balloon - nothing was left... (She cries) Nothing.

SON. Don't cry Mummy, I'll get you an even bigger belly.

MOTHER. (Smiles behind her tears) Never mind, my loves, never mind. Because do you know what happened then?

SON. What?

MOTHER. Then... then... you appeared.

SON. (Very surprised) ME!

MOTHER. Yes love; you came straight out of my belly. You

were in it - you <u>were</u> my belly. My son, my hero, my sweet sun...

DAUGHTER. What about me?

MOTHER. (Dismissively) Oh you, you came later.

DAUGHTER. I came from Daddy's belly?

MOTHER. No, no. You came from my belly as well. All, all came from my belly.

SON. (Excited) Daddy too?

DAUGHTER. Daddy came out of his mummy's belly.

MOTHER. It's the same thing, children, it's just the same.

SON. All came out of your belly?

MOTHER. Yes, yes. Mummy is everything in life, you know.

SON & DAUGHTER. Yes, yes.

MOTHER. I'm everything to you, aren't I?

SON & DAUGHTER. Right; right. We have got your presents, Mummy. Do you want to see them now?

MOTHER. Oh... but you shouldn't really.

SON & DAUGHTER. (Enthusaistically) Yes! Yes!

MOTHER. (Worried a little) You shouldn't... you really...

(CHILDREN run and fetch parcels. Hand them over to MOTHER. Then help her undo them. Inside are all sorts of household articles. Some in their normal size and shape, some distorted, some change as they are handed to MOTHER. E.g. the sweeping brush explodes like a gun, the saucepan suddenly gets heavy in her hand. She pours sand out of the teapot, a vase breaks as she takes it, etc. The procedure of giving the presents can be arranged in some kind of ceremonial pattern while the dialogue continues.)

SON & DAUGHTER. Here... here... another one... and another...

MOTHER. (Taking the presents) It's wonderful... wonderful... all my life, all my life is passing before my very eyes... Oh this... And this... you are wonderful. You love your poor old Mummy so much... More ... more.

SON & DAUGHTER. Here! Here!

MOTHER. My little angels... my angels.

SON & DAUGHTER. We gave you all of them. (They finish with the presents.)

MOTHER. Yes, yes. Now Mummy will give you something. What would you like Mummy to give you? Eh?

SON & DAUGHTER. Nothing, Mummy, nothing.

MOTHER. Just a little something. Eh?

SON & DAUGHTER. Everything, Mummy, everything.

MOTHER. I know what to give you, I always have. Here, take this. (She takes out a model of the room they are in and gives it to them.)

SON & DAUGHTER. But... what are we to do with it?

MOTHER. Practise, children , practise. You always wanted one, didn't you? (She hands them puppets.) That's Mummy, that's Daddy, and that's Granny and this is you and you... Take them and practise, so that you'll be prepared for life.

(SON and DAUGHTER take them, put the model in front of the bed and sit down by it.)

So that you'll be strong and beautiful and wise...

(SON and DAUGHTER begin to take the puppets apart laughing and giggling with pleasure.)

SON. (Laughs) That's Daddy.

DAUGHTER. (Laughs) That's Mummy.

MOTHER. (Looks at them lovingly) Everything is for you...

SON & DAUGHTER. ... and that's Grandmother.

MOTHER. I have so much hope in you...

SON. (To DAUGHTER) And that's you...

MOTHER. I gave up everything for you.

DAUGHTER. (To SON) And that's you.

MOTHER. I've sacrificed all my life for you, for my family, my children...

(By now the CHILDREN have finished taking the puppets apart. They sit motionless, their heads towards MOTHER, eyes open wide.)

But it was worth it, yes all was worth it... (She looks at the CHILDREN. A pause. Then) One day you'll leave me... I know... I'll be left alone... I won't be able to be a mother any more... Oh! I want more than anything to have my wonderful belly once more, once more, just once. All of you, my family, my flesh and blood, you are all so close to me, so like me, you are me, myself, myself; all of you... (She slowly gets up off the bed; looks around) It was a wonderful party... they were all so sweet... they must have been preparing for it for such a long time. They put such great effort and thought and feeling into it... they are really wonderful... my darlings... (She looks around, slowly takes off her dressing gown, remains in a thin nightdress, goes over to the dressing table... and looks in the mirror. All her movements are now very slow as if in slow-motion.

Lights change. Looking in the mirror) What do I look like?

How awful! (She starts to make herself up. The telephone rings and glows. She goes over to it, picks up the receiver.) Hallo... oh, it's you, Eric... Yes, it's me... What?... Oh no, not tonight, my husband, you know... Tomorrow... Yes, chez vous... ciao! Eric. (She puts the receiver down. The doorbell rings in a peculiar way. She calls very sweetly) Who's there?

MAN'S VOICE. The postman.

MOTHER. (Seductively) Coming. (She glances once more at the mirror, loosens her nightdress a little, wets her lips, smiles and goes out.

No one moves on stage, but of course they see and 'understand' everything.

After a short while, MOTHER re-enters, smiles to herself. Pause.

Suddenly GRANDMOTHER makes a peculiar noise. MOTHER starts, looks around. No one moves. Pause. She calms down. A pause.

SON makes another peculiar noise. FATHER groans, she starts again, looks around, they stop, she calms down.)

FATHER. (Groaning, then slowly, without moving, begins to talk) Who was it?

MOTHER. (Jumps) Ha?

FATHER. (Threatening her) On the phone, dear, on the phone!

MOTHER. What?

FATHER. The letters, the little notes, the whisperings, the secret meetings...

MOTHER. But...

SON. Why do you go to the cafe every day?

MOTHER. (Jumps) Wha...

DAUGHTER. Why do you leave us alone every day?

GRANDMOTHER. Why do you treat me like dirt?

MOTHER. But I...

GRANDMOTHER. Filth!

FATHER. What are you doing? What are you doing?

GRANDMOTHER. Look at the way you treat your husband.

FATHER. What are you doing to your children?

SON & DAUGHTER. Do you want to kill us?

MOTHER. (Shouts) I don't...

FATHER. Monster!

GRANDMOTHER. Whore!

> (During the following dialogue they get up and approach her. Their movement must not be realistic. They crawl on the floor growling, then get up, move on and freeze suddenly etc. She retreats towards the bed, falls on it, they jump on her.)

SON. Why didn't you let me play with the other children when I wanted to?

DAUGHTER. Why didn't you let me sleep with boys when I wanted to?

FATHER. Why didn't you let me go to America?

GRANDMOTHER. Why didn't you buy me nice dresses?

MOTHER. It was... It was...

SON. Why did you lock me in the lavatory?

FATHER. Why didn't you give anything up?

SON. Why did you build such great hopes for us?

DAUGHTER. Make me go to High School?

SON. Why did you let me go around in wet nappies?

FATHER. Didn't let me smoke.

SON. Suck!

FATHER. Drink!

GRANDMOTHER. Pray!

MOTHER. (Bewildered) Out of love, darlings! Out of love.

ALL. What love!

GRANDMOTHER. Do you love yourMother and Father?

FATHER. Your husband?

SON & DAUGHTER. Your children?

MOTHER. Yes! Yes! I love! I love!

FATHER. Do you love eating?

SON. Do you love sleeping?

DAUGHTER. Do you love shitting?

GRANDMOTHER. Do you love beating?

ALL. Us? Us?

SON. Do you love porridge?

DAUGHTER. Do you love spinach?

FATHER. Do you love jackets?

GRANDMOTHER. Do you love strait jackets?

MOTHER. (Shouts) I love! I love! I love!

FATHER. Why do you think there's evil in the world?

SON. Why are all these wars in the world?

DAUGHTER. Exploitation!

GRANDMOTHER. Lust!

SON & DAUGHTER. Degradation!

FATHER. Hate!

GRANDMOTHER. Hate!

ALL. Kill! Kill! Kill!

MOTHER. Love! Love! ... Out of love! Only love! All is love! In love, with love, to love, from love, by love, give love, get love, only love, love, love, love!

ALL. (As if they were barking) Hove, hove, hove.

(She is in bed. They are very close to her now.)

MOTHER. Come to me, my love, come love, come, come to me, come to me.

ALL. We are coming, we are coming!

MOTHER. Come with love, out of love, to love!

(They jump on the bed)

All is love, all is...

(They cover her with their bodies. A pause. She gets out from under their bodies, slowly crawls to the foot of the bed, then begins to speak, facing the audience. She is very weak when she starts, but has regained her strength by the end of the speech.)

Never mind, never mind, it's all out of love... Now I know you really love me as much as I love you. Now we can really be united... as we should... As I always hoped it would be... Nothing will stand between us, nothing... and it will be so easy, so simple. You will be mine, all of you... and I'll be yours, I'll be everything to you, all you have, all you are... I'll be all... at last... I'll bear you again, and again, and again...

(She looks around, love on her face, in her eyes, in her voice, she smiles with love.)

It was the most beautiful Mother's day I've ever had.

(Pause. Light fades slowly, a last spot remains for a brief moment on the scattered pieces of the model and the puppets on the floor, and fades.)

THE IDEAL FAMILY

(a biblical tale)

or, What would Dr Freud have said about it?
and, in addition, a few words by Grandmother.

Characters
FATHER
MOTHER
SON
DAUGHTER
GRANDMOTHER

(The dining room. The table is set. As the curtain rises
the stage is empty. After ten seconds the sound of front
door being opened and closed. Immediately a woman's
voice is heard calling cheerfully and excitedly.)

MOTHER. (Calling off) Tiger!

FATHER. (From the kitchen, cheerfully) In the kitchen
kitty.

(Enter MOTHER. She wears a man's suit and holds a
man's briefcase. She puts it down and takes off her
jacket.)

MOTHER. Dinner ready?

FATHER. (From the kitchen, cheerfully) In a minute, my
angel.

MOTHER. Super, you rogue. Just going to wash.

FATHER. Take your time, Peachy Pie.

(MOTHER exits to bathroom.)

MOTHER. (From the bathroom) Plum-Plum home yet?

FATHER. Not yet, Honey.

(Sound of front door.)

Is that you, Plum?

SON'S VOICE. Yes it's me, Baby.

(SON enters. He is very manly. He looks around, notices MOTHER's jacket and briefcase, and sits down.)

SON. (Calls) Mother home?

FATHER. Yes, Chuchy-Pooh.

(MOTHER enters.)

MOTHER. (To SON, lovingly) Hello, Pot.

SON. (To MOTHER, same tone) Hello, Gorilla.

(FATHER enters from kitchen, carrying a tray with plates to the table. He wears a dress and an apron. His manner may be described as soft and gentle, but not 'camp'.)

FATHER. (Cheerfully) All on time, loveys. Let's start.

(They sit. FATHER serves and sits too)

Oh, it's so wonderful! Aren't we lucky?

(They all smile affectionately at each other and start to eat.)

Nice?

MOTHER. (While eating, appreciatively) Mmmmm.

FATHER. (To SON) Taste good?

SON. (As MOTHER) Mmmmm.

(They eat.)

FATHER. (To MOTHER) How was the office today?

MOTHER. (Eating) Mmmmmm.

FATHER. (To SON) Staying in this evening?

SON. (Eating) Mmmmm.

(They finish eating and get up. FATHER removes the dishes. MOTHER takes a newspaper and sits in an armchair. SON goes to radio and turns it on. Music.)

MOTHER. (Behind the paper) Sh - sh... you little devil. (SON turns down the volume) How was school today?

SON. All right. Coming to football on Sunday, Mother?

MOTHER. O.K. But Father will have to give up his visit to Grandmother.

SON. Pop's a darling. He won't mind.

MOTHER. All right then.

(She looks at him tenderly, smiles, he smiles back)

It really pleases me that you have so much respect for your Father. I had a great deal for my Father.

(SON nods and smiles. She smiles back. There is a feeling of sheer happiness.

FATHER enters from kitchen, taking off his apron.)

FATHER. (To MOTHER) What would you like to do this evening, Mother?

MOTHER. I don't know, love. Had a hell of a day.

34

FATHER. You work too hard, dear.

MOTHER. I don't mind. I know it is for the good of all of us.

FATHER. You really are wonderful.

> (They smile to each other with affection and understanding. To SON)

> Would you take the rubbish downstairs before you go to bed, Dimply-Doo?

SON. Of course, Snooky-Snooks. (He goes towards the door.) Nighty-nighty.

FATHER. Pyjama- Pyjama.

> (Exit SON. To MOTHER)

> You know, he's a wonderful son. After lunch he washed all the dishes by himself.

MOTHER. Yes, he's an extraordinary child.

FATHER. He treats me as if I were his Mother.

MOTHER. (Smiles with understanding) Yes, he's a real man.

FATHER. Oh, there is just one thing that worries me about him.

MOTHER. What's that?

FATHER. He doesn't masturbate any more.

MOTHER. Hm-mmm.

FATHER. And he goes out with girls. (MOTHER looks at him with interest.) A lot.

MOTHER. Well...

FATHER. And I have found a packet of johnnies in his trousers.

MOTHER. Oh! (Short pause) That's a bit much. (Short pause) I'll have a word with him. (She yawns) I am really very tired. Come, let's go to bed, squirrel.

FATHER. O.K.

(They get up and go towards the bedroom. FATHER stops to put out the light.)

MOTHER. You know what? I think I'd like another baby. Perhaps a girl... what do you think?

FATHER. (Smiles with understanding) Whenever you like, Lion.

MOTHER. (Smiles) Come to bed, Weasel.

(They exit.

Blackout. Lights up. It is morning. MOTHER sits at the table drinking her coffee and reading a newspaper. Behind the table sits the DAUGHTER, a pretty girl of about 17. She wears a baby's dress, but her way of talking and behaviour befit her actual age. The SON enters with a tray. He wears a woman's dressing gown.)

SON. (To MOTHER) Good morning, darling. (He kisses her and puts the tray on the table.)

MOTHER. Good morning, dear.

SON. Do you want some toast?

MOTHER. (Finishes her coffee) No, thank you - I'm late already. I'll have something at the office.

(She puts down the paper, gets up, kisses the DAUGHTER on the forehead. The DAUGHTER does not react at all. The MOTHER goes towards the front door. SON goes with her, takes her briefcase and hands it to her at the door.)

SON. Are you coming home for lunch, Mother?

MOTHER. Yes.

SON. Pity Father didn't live to see all this. It would have made him very happy.

MOTHER. Yes, it's a great shame. Poor Daddy. It was a rough birth for him.

(She looks at DAUGHTER. Then kisses SON.)

See you then. Bye-bye.

SON. Bye, love.

(MOTHER exits. SON goes back to the table, sees that DAUGHTER hasn't touched any food at all. Sympathetically)

Why aren't you eating?

DAUGHTER. I hate her guts.

SON. What a way to talk.

DAUGHTER. How can you stand all this? How do you bear it?

SON. Why shouldn't I?

DAUGHTER. Just look at yourself in that pansy dress!

SON. Still the same old story. Why should it bother you so much? She's our breadwinner, and someone has to look after the house, so why shouldn't I?

DAUGHTER. You... are a man.

SON. So what of it?

DAUGHTER. You should be the breadwinner.

SON. Oh stuff! Who says?

DAUGHTER. The Bible.

SON. Prejudice.

DAUGHTER. You make me sick.

SON. (Begins to clear the table) I just don't understand you sometimes. You are so odd. We have always lived like this. Father used to do the housework so it is up to me to carry on.

DAUGHTER. (Slowly, in a low voice and with great hatred) She - killed - him.

(A pause.)

SON. Have you gone out of your mind?

DAUGHTER. She killed him - I know she did.

SON. My God, you really are nuts.

DAUGHTER. I know she did it.

SON. It was just a difficult birth, that's all.

DAUGHTER. Yeah, that's what she told you. I saw it.

SON. You...

DAUGHTER. Yes.

SON. When?

DAUGHTER. Night time.

SON. Night time?

DAUGHTER. Yes... the same night I was born. I was there. I saw it all. First she put her arms round him, lay on top of him, covering him with her body. He tried to turn over, got her on her back, but she trapped him with her legs and twisted him over again. They scratched and bit at each other. Oh, it was horrible! He fought fought, he breathed harder, he tried to turn her over again but she held him with her legs like a huge octopus, then she put her hands on his neck, her mouth on his, he couldn't breathe, but she kept on and on, and then... and then... she choked him to death.

SON. No, no, you are lying. It can't be true. He had a hard birth, that's all. He was too sensitive, it was just a hard birth...

DAUGHTER. You are a coward.

SON. Shut up.

DAUGHTER. I am so ashamed... so ashamed.

SON. Shut your mouth.

DAUGHTER. You are his son. You should have revenged him.

SON. Shut up, you're crazy. You are out of your mind.

DAUGHTER. I won't shut up.

SON. (Shouts) If you don't shut up I will come and make you!

DAUGHTER. (Laughs) Come on, come on then, muscles. Come and get me. Make me shut up. Come and make me. I am waiting. I am just waiting for you to make me. Come on, get me! Make me! Come on, come on... come... come...

(Towards the end of her speech SON gets nearer and nearer to her, then stops... A pause. He looks at her and starts to laugh)

SON. You are jealous... Yes, you are jealous of her, that's it. Jealous, jealous, jealous.

DAUGHTER. Yes! I AM jealous. So what? Why shouldn't I be? She has no right to treat you like that. Look what she is doing to you. You are a man. You are a great big hunk of a man.

SON. What do you want of me?

DAUGHTER. You could have any girl you want. You could have a real girl, a nice bit of stuff, with firm young breasts and milk-white thighs.

SON. What do you want of me?

DAUGHTER. You can have ANY girl, any girl... any girl.

SON. (Shouts) What do you want of me?

DAUGHTER. (Slowly) You can have me.

(Pause)

SON. You?

(Pause)

DAUGHTER. Yes, me.

SON. And her?

DAUGHTER. She's just an old bag. She's had it.

(Short pause)

SON. You.

DAUGHTER. Yes.

SON. Right.

DAUGHTER. Tonight?

SON. Tonight!

DAUGHTER. And she did kill him, anyway. It serves her right.

(A quick blackout.

Lights up. It is evening. The table is set for two. After a second, the sound of the front door, and SON's voice)

SON. Anybody home?

DAUGHTER'S VOICE. Yes, darling love. I am in the kitchen.

(Enter SON. He wears a suit very similar to MOTHER's suit. He puts down his briefcase and goes to the table.)

DAUGHTER. (Off) Do start, Honeypot. I'm just coming.

SON. (Sits at the table) O.K. Mummy. (He starts to eat) How do you feel today?

DAUGHTER. Great, Daddy. Have you started?

SON. Yes, it's very nice.

DAUGHTER. I made it specially.

SON. (Eating) You are a much better cook than Mother.

(DAUGHTER laughs.)

DAUGHTER. Honestly?

(DAUGHTER enters with a dish. She is obviously pregnant.)

SON. You are as big as a horse.

DAUGHTER. Don't laugh. I think it must be an elephant.

SON. (Laughs) If not worse.

DAUGHTER. (Giggles) Don't be mean. It could happen any minute now.

SON. I hope so. I'm dying to see what it is.

DAUGHTER. Oh, it's sure to be wonderful. With your beauty and my brains or vice-versa, upside down, inside out, back to front, and arse to tit.

(She starts her pains)

Oh...oo...oo. Oh...oo...ohhh.

SON. What is it?

DAUGHTER. It's started... Oh! Call a taxi... Oh! Oh!
Quickly, get me to the hospital. Oh, it's coming, it's
coming!

SON. Oh, yes... right, my God, what... yes...

DAUGHTER. It's coming, it's coming.

SON. Yes ma-ma... yes, mater.

(SON leads DAUGHTER to the door.)

DAUGHTER. Switch off the light.

(SON rushes to put out the lights. Blackout.

Lights go up. It is daytime. There is a playpen on stage
and inside it is GRANDMOTHER. She is very old, but
dressed like a baby. Her speech and behaviour are very
aggressive. SON and DAUGHTER are sitting at the table.)

GRANDMOTHER. (Shouts) Let me out! Let me out of here!

SON. (To DAUGHTER) O God! She's at it again.

DAUGHTER. (To GRANDMOTHER) Don't cry, my little
Angel, don't cry.

GRANDMOTHER. I'm not crying. I'm screaming! Let me
out! Let... me... out of here! Ou-out!

DAUGHTER. You can't come out of your playpen, little
beastie. You are just a tiny tot, you can't even walk.

GRANDMOTHER. I can't walk because I'm too bloody old -
not because I'm a tiny bloody tot. You can't keep me in
this cage like a baby. I am not a baby - I am your
GRANDMOTHER.

SON. Perhaps she is hungry.

42

DAUGHTER. Of course you are hungry, ickle piggy. Mummy will give you something to eat.

(She gives her a bottle with a teat. GRANDMOTHER aggressively throws it away.)

GRANDMOTHER. You do it on purpose! All you do is torture me. You wish I was dead.

DAUGHTER. She has lost her appetite. It must be a year since she had anything to eat. Nothing since she was born in fact.

SON. All she does is scream. Why can't she stop it? It's driving me mad.

GRANDMOTHER. You are sick of me! I am too old, that's what. You are sick and tired of looking after me, washing me, dressing me, wiping my arse. You can't fool me. You want to torture me to death.

SON. Just listen to the way she screams.

DAUGHTER. (To GRANDMOTHER) How dare you raise your voice like that to your Mother and Father.

GRANDMOTHER. Piss off! You are not my Mother and Father. I'm your rotten Grandmother.

SON. Oh, bloody hell, shut her up. Pick her up and shake her or something.

DAUGHTER. It isn't good for her. The doctor says you shouldn't do that every time she cries. Its a bad habit.

GRANDMOTHER. You are a pair of lying, cheating crooks, that's what you are.

SON. I can't take any more of it.

GRANDMOTHER. I know all about you. I know everything you have done. I'm not just a pissing little baby. I know it all. You are rotten right through.

SON. I can't bear it any more.

GRANDMOTHER. You incestuous monsters.

SON. Just listen to the way she goes on.

DAUGHTER. What can I do?

GRANDMOTHER. Murderers!

SON. Shut your gob.

DAUGHTER. You make her shut up.

SON. It was your idea in the first place.

DAUGHTER. It's as much your responsibility.

GRANDMOTHER. (Shouts) Criminals!

SON. Who put this curse on me?

DAUGHTER. You did yourself.

SON. You bitch! Don't you blame me.

DAUGHTER. Yes, that's it... shout... go ahead... shout your head off. Let all the neighbours hear.

SON. I'll shout as loud as I want to. I'll shout as loud as I can. I'll shout it from the housetops. I'll tell the world, Electra!

DAUGHTER. Oedipus!

SON. Adultress!

DAUGHTER. Pervert!

SON. I warn you!

DAUGHTER. Murderer!

SON. I'll tear you to bits!

DAUGHTER. I'll scratch your eyes out!

SON. I'll bash your brains in!

DAUGHTER. I'll tear your guts out!

> (They jump on each other and the light goes down.
>
> When the lights come up GRANDMOTHER is sitting in an armchair wearing a dressing gown and spectacles, knitting a baby's dress.)

GRANDMOTHER. (Very calmly and slowly, as if telling a story) After Cain killed Abel, Adam and Eve had a third son, whom they called Shet, and Shet begat Anush, but how did he do it? There was only Eve around then, according to the Bible, wasn't there? (She laughs and winks) Well, shall we start all over again...
(She laughs.)

THE COLLECTORS

Characters
FATHER
MOTHER
SON
DAUGHTER
GRANDMOTHER

(The living room. In various places around the room
arranged in an orderly manner there are various
collections of different things. E.g. china, glass, etc.

As the curtain rises, MOTHER, GRANDMOTHER,
DAUGHTER and SON are on stage. MOTHER cleans
her nails with a nail file, DAUGHTER is squeezing her
spots, GRANDMOTHER picks her nose, SON cleans his
ear with his finger. They busy themselves peacefully
for 30 seconds, then for no obvious reason and without
expression they get up and leave the stage one by one.
Silence. The stage is empty for 30 seconds.

Sound of front door. Enter FATHER carrying some
parcels.)

FATHER. Anybody home?

(Enter MOTHER, GRANDMOTHER, SON and DAUGHTER)

Of course, there is never anybody home.

(Exit ALL, except FATHER.)

What a way to live! A man comes home in the evening
exhausted after a hard day's work, or after doing

46

absolutely nothing - which is even more exhausting, and what does he find? A jungle full of animals! And what do all these animals do? They lick one another by day and bite each other by night. A man expects to find some warmth, some tenderness, some kind of understanding, at least in his own home, but what does he get instead? STINK! (Shouts) Why doesn't somebody clean this bloody cess-pit from time to time? Why doesn't somebody clean the lavatory for a change?

(Enter MOTHER by the front door, carrying some nicely wrapped parcels. GRANDMOTHER enters from bedroom and goes over to her armchair. SON enters and crosses to the cupboard, takes out two drawers and puts them down beside GRANDMOTHER. Enter DAUGHTER with an album. FATHER looks at them.)

FATHER. This whole place stinks. Do you hear me? It stinks!

(They resume their previous places and their 'business' of the opening of the scene. Then they all scratch.

Exit FATHER to dining room. SON goes over to MOTHER. She looks in his ears.)

MOTHER. There's a good boy. No potatoes in your ears?

DAUGHTER. I lost my virginity this afternoon.

MOTHER. Did you go horse-riding?

DAUGHTER. No.

MOTHER. Did you fall on a stick?

DAUGHTER. No.

MOTHER. So how do you know?

SON. I checked.

MOTHER. Oh, well - did you jump out of a plane?

DAUGHTER. No, they jumped on me.

MOTHER. Who?

DAUGHTER. Three nasty vicious men. They attacked me
as I came out of school. They flung me on the ground,
tore my dress. One of them was pulling my hair.
Another one pulled my legs apart and the third one did
it. He chopped me in two. The blade went through me
like a hot iron. Then the others - oh, by then I was
flowing like a river. Everything was pouring out of me.
Then they left me crawling on the ground, earth in my
eyes, earth between my legs. I could hardly get up.
With my last strength I got to the policeman who was
on the corner of the street and he helped me to cross
the road.

(A short pause)

MOTHER. Good girl, there is a lot of traffic on the road
these days.

(MOTHER starts to unwrap her parcels. GRAND-
MOTHER takes some table napkins from one of the
two drawers which are beside her, which she examines
with great care, folding them and putting them in the
other drawer.

Enter FATHER through the front door, carrying some
parcels.

Exit CHILDREN.)

FATHER. I don't understand how there can possibly be anyone who doesn't realise the value of collecting. (He
puts down some of his parcels) After handling people all
day it's such a relief to deal with something real. It
gives you a feeling of security. It's something utterly
dependable. It gives meaning to one's life.

(He exits with some of his parcels to the bedroom.)

MOTHER. (As if he was still in the room) How right you
are. I keep telling the children the same thing day and

night.

(Enter FATHER from the front door.)

FATHER. Everything is against me. Everything.

(Exit MOTHER and GRANDMOTHER.)

Yes. I haven't a soul in the world. At the office they all laugh at me. I muck up everything and nobody cares. I send all incoming mail out and throw away all outgoing mail. I lose the Company thousands of pounds and no - one takes any notice. I call the boss a cross-eyed spastic. I order the scretary to copy out every letter fifty times by hand and in different colours. I order the tea-boy to count the grains of sugar he puts in my tea, and if he does it wrong I beat him with my belt - and what happens? They all grin at me and are even nicer to me... I can't go on like this - I just can't go on like this any more!

(He exits.

Thirty seconds' silence. The stage is empty. A clock strikes three, then five, then two, then eight, then goes wild. Silence.

Enter GRANDMOTHER. She goes to her armchair. Sits down and goes back to her napkins. Enter MOTHER by the front door, carrying more parcels and a carrier bag containing foodstuff. She goes to the kitchen.)

MOTHER. (Crossing the room, excitedly, to GRANDMOTHER) You'll never guess what I got today, Grandmother. (She goes to the kitchen, while continuing her speech, leaves the bag there and re-enters with her parcels.) It will be the most gorgeous of them all. I fell head over heels in love with it at first sight. (She unwraps one of the parcels and takes out a coloured cardboard cut-out figure.) For years I prayed for one like this of my very own. Oh, it's so marvellous!

GRANDMOTHER. I have been tidying up the old napkins...

MOTHER. And just look at this. (She unwraps another parcel.)

GRANDMOTHER. They should be seen to regularly. They get lonely if they are not seen to regularly.

MOTHER. (Taking out one long hair) Look! Look! How tiny it is...

GRANDMOTHER. We knew how to treat them in the old days.

MOTHER. Touch it... feel it... it's, it's almost... nonexistent.

GRANDMOTHER. (Taking it) My Mother, God rest her soul, she used to collect hair. I am so glad you collect it too. It bodes well. It shows you have true family feeling and when you're my age you will collect napkins, tablecloths and sheets... Did you bring me the sheets I asked for?

MOTHER. Oh yes. (She undoes one of the parcels and hands some sheets to GRANDMOTHER) These are the biggest I could get. If you like them you can have them by the hundred tomorrow.

GRANDMOTHER. (Takes the sheets) This is my favourite collection. Soft, clean, pure. (She smells them) They smell like the old house. Your father used to collect sheets too. He had the best collection I've ever seen...

(SON bursts in excitedly, holding insignia and badges of every description. On his jacket he has got some medals, badges and army insignia.)

SON. (Pointing at his medals) The Battle of Britain. The Battle of Trafalgar. The Battle of Hastings...

MOTHER. Eh?...

SON. (Opens his jacket. It is virtually covered with all sorts of insignia, labels, signs and buttons. Among them: 3d off. Buy now. New economy size. Squeeze me. Lassie makes dogs bounce with health. Carnation milk

50

made from contented cows. Shake before using. I'm
sexy. I'm a virgin. I'm your man. He points at some
of them one after another.) Carnation milk made from
contented cows; squeeze me; I'm sexy; buy now; Lassie
makes dogs bounce with health...

(MOTHER laughs, enjoying the performance. DAUGHTER
enters from the children's room, holding an album. She
is nearly crying.)

DAUGHTER. (Tears in her eyes) I can't find my little worms.

MOTHER. Don't cry my pet. You must take more care of
your things.

DAUGHTER. (Crying) I did! I did! I can't find them.

SON. (Points to another button) I'm your man. Follow me.

(SON goes to door followed by DAUGHTER. She goes
out first. Before his exit he turns to MOTHER.)

She'll never learn.

(Exit.)

GRANDMOTHER. When I was a young girl I used to collect
boxes. My Grandmother used to collect boxes too. We
had a house full of boxes. My Grandfather collected
cardboard. It was very rare in those days, it made him
rich.

(Enter FATHER with parcels. He crosses the room to
the bedroom and exits.

Enter SON and DAUGHTER happy. SON speaks.)

SON. (Proudly) We've found them! We've found them.
(Takes off one of his medals and replaces it on the
other side of his jacket.) The Battle of Worms.

MOTHER. (To SON) Well done dear. As your Father always
says, the great art of collecting stimulates the
imagination and brings us to terms with reality.

51

QUEEN MARGARET COLLEGE LIBRARY

(Enter FATHER.)

MOTHER. (To FATHER) That's what you always say, isn't it dear?

FATHER. (Speaks gruffly) Mm...mm...mm.

(Exit FATHER.

MOTHER looks at GRANDMOTHER, who shrugs her shoulders and returns to her collection.)

SON. I would like to start a new collection, Mummy.

MOTHER. That's nice... What?

SON. Leaves.

MOTHER. Leaves? Well... it's very educational.

(Re-enter FATHER, bringing with him all kinds of swords, rifles, a guillotine and nooses. They all look at him.)

Your collection has come along very nicely dear.

FATHER. You have no idea what I'm up to. This is no collection. This is to be the greatest achievement of my life.

SON. (Getting excited) I'm going to collect grass too.

MOTHER. (With decision) I shall start to collect pictures, antiques, library books...

DAUGHTER. I... I... I'll collect animals...

SON. And I'll collect... Trees... land...

DAUGHTER. Dogs, cats, monkies...

SON. What else?

GRANDMOTHER. I want bubblegum!

52

MOTHER. And television sets, washing machines, electric...

(Simultaneously)

DAUGHTER. Err... donkies and mice, ants, grubs, fleas...

MOTHER. Telephones.

SON. Yes, deserts, oceans...

(Simultaneously)

DAUGHTER. Cows, cubes, spiders, circles...

MOTHER. Squares.

SON. Queers.

DAUGHTER. Hands, legs, fingers.

SON. What else?

MOTHER. Neuroses.

DAUGHTER. Toes.

SON. What else?

MOTHER. More! More!

ALL. More... More... More... More...

(And simultaneously -)

DAUGHTER. Earth...

SON. Water...

MOTHER. Fire...

DAUGHTER. Air...

ALL. We collect! We collect!

(They all, except FATHER rush out in different
directions. GRANDMOTHER is trying to catch up.)

GRANDMOTHER. (On her way out) I want bubble-gum.

(Exits)

FATHER. (Calls after them) Fools! You miserable fools!
What are all your collections in comparison to this?
Trash! I've had them all. I know how worthless, how
pointless they all are. But now, here, what power,
what meaning.

(He returns to his collection)

With this rifle they executed twenty-five cowards during
the Thirty Years War. With this great sword Ivan the
Terrible executed five hundred and forty seven Boyars,
with this guillotine they decapitated three thousand six
hundred and thirty nine royalists in the Reign of Terror,
and with this rope they hanged the Arizona Kid. Oh, you
magical, magnificent instruments of death. Even those
who used you so fearlessly couldn't understand your
true meaning. But I can. Not what you did, but what -
together, you are! My own body is decaying and rotting
but here before me is the power over death itself. In
front of me are the Spanish Inquisition, Billy the Kid,
the Nazi Gestapo, Freud, Human Sacrifices to the Gods,
Batman, Jack the Ripper. I dream I am tortured, on the
rack, poisoned, burned alive . I see my body cut to
pieces, burning cigarettes pushed into my seared soles,
razor-blades stuck under my nails, a great knife
hacking my limbs, my limbs torn from my body one by
one and eaten by vultures and wolves while my blood is
pouring and spurting out of them, spreading all over the
earth...

(ALL rush in, one after the other. First SON carrying
a couple of boxes, emptying their contents onto the floor.
Screws, nails etc. Enter MOTHER with rolls of cloth
which she puts on the floor and folds. DAUGHTER next
with pots and pans. While crossing room she trips over
SON's collection.)

DAUGHTER. Sorry.

SON. It's all right.

DAUGHTER. Thank you.

(FATHER brings in an electric chair.)

MOTHER. There's a space here.

FATHER. Hmmm...

MOTHER. Don't mention it.

(Enter GRANDMOTHER)

GRANDMOTHER. I've got some bubble-gum.

(They busy themselves arranging their collections for a while.)

I want more bubble-gum.

FATHER. (Impatiently) Not again.

MOTHER. Really Granny, didn't we give you enough yesterday?

GRANDMOTHER. (Complaining) Nobody cares about me. You know I can't go out any more, so I have to ask you to bring me my bubble-gum. But you only get things for yourselves, only for yourselves!

SON. (Impatiently) What is she on about now?

MOTHER. (To SON) Stop that, how dare you?

(He shrugs his shoulders and exits to a nearby room.

To GRANDMOTHER)

You know it isn't true, Mother, we are always thinking about you, but we have to collect a lot and fast and we just haven't the time...

(Noticing SON is not in his place she hesitates for a moment and surreptitiously puts some of her stuff in his place.)

MOTHER. (To GRANDMOTHER) You must understand.

GRANDMOTHER. You're all selfish. You'll come to a
   sticky end.

(SON brings in various boxes, crates, etc.)

MOTHER. (Surprised, to SON) What's all that?

SON. Use your eyes. Boxes, crates, cases, tins, barrels,
   anything which contains space, it will be a collection
   of the infinite, the true conquest of space!

(While he talks he brings in more stuff and in doing so
he bumps into DAUGHTER's collection.)

DAUGHTER. Watch where you're going!

SON. Did you say something?

DAUGHTER. You stepped on my collection.

SON. (Contemptuously) Huh! You call this a collection?

(SON begins to put his stuff in order, proudly. The
PARENTS watch him then look at each other and return
to arrange their own collections with greater urgency.

DAUGHTER looks at him too then goes out.)

FATHER. When I was a young lad I had the whole world at
   my feet. Yes sir, I had a different girl every day, two,
   three, four girls in one night. Three, four, five, seven,
   ten times every one of them. Liquor, drugs, gambling,
   the lot!

(DAUGHTER re-enters, brings various household things.
She goes to put them near SON.)

SON. This space is occupied!

DAUGHTER. What do you mean?

SON. Occupied! Occupied!

56

DAUGHTER. Bastard.

(She crosses to another place with her things. On her way one of her things falls onto her MOTHER's territory.)

MOTHER. (Shouts) Watch out!

(DAUGHTER picks up the thing, goes to her place, puts her things down and unintentionally touches some of the SON's things.)

SON. (Shouts) Watch it!

FATHER. (Engaged in his collection) With this very axe they chopped off the head of Mary, Queen of Scots.

(SON brings some more boxes in and spreads them near to DAUGHTER.)

DAUGHTER. (To SON, nervously) Don't come near me!

SON. What's the matter with you? I only want to help.

DAUGHTER. Leave me alone.

(MOTHER sees clash between DAUGHTER and SON and takes the opportunity to sneak out unnoticed.)

SON. Don't get worked up, it's for your own good. You have to be taught how to collect.

DAUGHTER. (Hysterically) Go away!

SON. All right. All right. You'll be screaming for help in a minute. I'm just waiting for it.

(MOTHER re-enters bringing lavatory seats of all sorts.)

What's that?

MOTHER. W.C., bog, loo, john, latrine, toilet, men's, gents, ladies, women's and little girls' room. Lavatory seats! Can't you see for yourself?

FATHER. It stinks! The whole place stinks! Can't you collect something that doesn't smell so much?

MOTHER. Listen to him. If this place stinks, it stinks because of the corpses you fill it with.

(SON sneaks out.)

FATHER. You damned fool. You don't have the faintest idea what I'm up to.

(SON brings in more boxes.)

MOTHER. (To SON) That's the limit! You're filling the house with empty boxes and cases all full of nothing at all, while we need all the space that we can get for real things.

SON. Nothing, eh? Well, I've got news for you, old girl: I'm collecting space, and that means I'm collecting all space, even the space you are in. Got it?

(FATHER brings in a corpse.)

MOTHER & SON. Good God, what's that?

FATHER. The body of Al Capone.

SON. Take it away.

FATHER. How dare you talk to me like that!

SON. It stinks.

FATHER. You stink.

MOTHER. Take it away!

FATHER. (To SON) Who taught you to collect when you were just a stinking little pig? Who taught you everything you know about collecting?

(DAUGHTER brings in more things and puts some in MOTHER's territory.)

MOTHER. (To DAUGHTER) Get this rubbish out of my space.

DAUGHTER. Shut your bloody mouth.

(SON brings in more stuff.)

FATHER. (To SON) Watch it!

MOTHER. (To DAUGHTER) I'll teach you. (She brings in more stuff.)

SON. (To FATHER) Mind your own business.

(They all push one another, and shout and fight.)

MOTHER. Get this thing out of my way.

SON. (To MOTHER) It's my place.

MOTHER. Bastard!

(DAUGHTER brings in more things. SON tries to block her way.)

DAUGHTER. Go away!

SON. You've got enough already.

(MOTHER and FATHER bring in more things, SON and DAUGHTER do the same. The battle has been getting more and more heated and reaches its climax at this point.)

MOTHER. Don't you dare touch my property!

FATHER. This is my place!

SON. Get your arse out of it!

DAUGHTER. Take your hands off me!

FATHER. You even cheated your own children!

MOTHER. Shut up!

SON. Whore!

DAUGHTER. Drop dead!

FATHER. Bitch!

MOTHER. Slob!

> (They reach a climax and GRANDMOTHER shouts)

GRANDMOTHER. I want more bubble-gum.

> (Immediate silence. They all stop dead in their tracks. They look at one another. Pause.)

FATHER. (Quietly) Somebody must give way.

> (Silence, To CHILDREN)

> You, get to your room.

SON. It's full up.

FATHER. (To MOTHER) What about the bedroom?

MOTHER. Full!

FATHER. The kitchen?

MOTHER. Full!

FATHER. The toilet?

MOTHER & CHILDREN. Full, full, full!

> (A pause.)

FATHER. (Very quietly) Someone will have to move.

GRANDMOTHER. I want more bubble-gum.

> (Silence. Everyone turns to her.)

FATHER. What did you say you wanted, Granny?

GRANDMOTHER. More bubble-gum.

FATHER. But you've got enough bubble-gum already, haven't you?

GRANDMOTHER. It's not enough. I want more. And I want more space for my bubble-gum.

FATHER. You've got your table cloths and your linen, why do you want more bubble-gum?

SON. Yes, it takes up a lot of very valuable space.

DAUGHTER. We're limiting ourselves as much as we can, but Grandmother wants more space.

FATHER. Well, what do you say, Mother?

MOTHER. I... I don't know...

FATHER. Don't you think Grandmother is expecting a bit much?

MOTHER. Well... yes.

(To GRANDMOTHER)

Why can't you be satisfied with just your linen, Mother?

GRANDMOTHER. I need more bubble-gum. And I need more space for my bubble-gum.

FATHER. See! Grandmother wants more space. Grandmother wants more and more space.

SON. The old bag doesn't know what she wants.

(They begin to approach GRANDMOTHER and surround her during the ensuing dialogue.)

FATHER. The old bag has a power complex.

DAUGHTER. She wants to rob us of the little space left to us.

MOTHER. Why not be satisfied with the place you have, Granny?

SON. Yes, you should be content with the enormous space you have already. It will be better for you.

FATHER. The old woman has no idea when to stop. She could die any minute but she wants more and more.

SON. She wants to expand at our expense.

DAUGHTER. On our expensive space.

FATHER. I think she takes up too much space herself.

SON. What do you say Mother?

MOTHER. I think she ought to be satisfied with the space she has.

DAUGHTER. It's too much for her anyway.

FATHER. If she gave up her space there would be more space for the rest of us... eh, Mother?

MOTHER. I think you're right.

FATHER. Now then! Mother thinks I am right as well.

SON. Right!

DAUGHTER. You take up too much precious space, Grandmother.

MOTHER. Yes. And we need all we can get.

FATHER. Well, Granny. Will you let us have some more space?

DAUGHTER. Will you give us _your_ space?

SON. Will you? Will you?

FATHER. Space! Space!

MOTHER. Space!

ALL. Space! Space! Space!

>(They are very close to her, surrounding her on all sides.)

GRANDMOTHER. I want more bubble-gum! More space! More...

>(They jump on top of her, push her down into the linen and wrap her in it. Short pause. They turn away from her. Another pause.)

MOTHER. She's dead.

>(Short pause)

FATHER. Really.

>(Short pause)

SON. What did she die of?

MOTHER. I can't bear it.

FATHER. (Sighs) Well, that's life.

SON. (To MOTHER) What's come over you?

FATHER. Funny.

SON. What?

FATHER. One minute you are full of beans and the next - poof! Just like that - poof! ...

MOTHER. (Nearly crying) She never even got the bubble-gum she wanted.

(Short pause)

DAUGHTER. (Cries) It's awful.

SON. She was very old.

FATHER. Yes, and she wasn't at all well.

MOTHER. You have no heart.

(Pause)

FATHER. We have got more space now.

(A pause. They all look towards GRANDMOTHER, then around them. Then at one another)

You know what?

SON. What?

FATHER. We must never forget what has happened.

MOTHER. What do you mean by that?

FATHER. It must not happen again.

DAUGHTER. What?

(Short pause)

FATHER. Never mind.

SON. Right.

(A pause)

MOTHER. What shall we do now?

(A pause. They all look towards GRANDMOTHER.)

FATHER. We shall erect a memorial.

ALL. (Very businesslike) Good.

(They raise GRANDMOTHER and put her on one of the boxes wrapped in a sheet, only her head is seen.)

FATHER. To a better world.

(They all bow their heads, raise them and look towards the empty space which GRANDMOTHER used to occupy. One by one they begin to shift some of their stuff into that place. It starts to develop into a new battle.)

Stop!

(Everybody stops.)

Oh no! We have learnt our lesson. We are not beasts, we still have the use of our reason, we must find a humane way. We are human beings, aren't we?

(He takes out a measuring tape. To SON)

Hold the end.

(They measure the empty space.)

This bit is mine, this bit's Mummy's, and this is yours. That's settled.

(They move some of their stuff to their new places and busy themselves with their stuff for a while.)

It's nice to be at home.

MOTHER. We are such a united family. We have a common interest that always made Grandmother proud.

(A short pause. All look at MOTHER.)

SON. Yes.

MOTHER. We are not just killing time.

FATHER. No, we have something that fills time for us.

DAUGHTER. I think I'll start to collect sheets.

(Short pause)

MOTHER. That would have made Grandmother very happy.

(A pause. They occupy themselves with their collections

I want bubble-gum.

(Pause. Everybody looks at her.)

FATHER. (Starts giggling) I once knew a man who called
himself TOP. One day this man met someone who
called himself POP. So they called themselves TOPOP.
I remember thinking at the time that this was a bit
strange. Some time later I know a man who was called
SAMMY. He met another man who was called SAMMY.
So they were called SAMMY SAMMY. This time I didn't
think it so strange. One day I met some people who
called themselves MOSSI. We had a lovely time.

(Family moves in towards FATHER)

One day we met someone. We called him MOSSI. But
he said that that wasn't his name. So we said to him:
That's what we call you. But he just stood there and
began to cut bits off himself which he gave to us.

(The family now begins to cut off FATHER's limbs,
beginning with his legs, until by the end of the story
only a torso remains.)

We said: give us more. He cut more and gave us more
and we cried out for more, until he was left with just
one eye. So we told him: that's your name. But he said:
No, that isn't my name and he took out his eye and gave
it to us.

(They finish cutting him up, cover him with a sheet so
only his head is showing. A brief pause and his head
drops. The three go back to their places with a part of
his body. They arrange themselves happily there and
reorganize their collections. Then...)

MOTHER. I want to collect all the bubble-gum in the world.

66

(A brief pause. She drops her head as FATHER did.
Another pause.)

SON. Collecting is... (SON drags his head in the same way.)

DAUGHTER. Sheets are my whole life. (She too drops her
head.

Pause. There is no movement for a second, then
FATHER lifts his head, looks straight ahead and says)

FATHER. I... I... I... I... (He drops his head.

There is no movement for about 30 seconds. A clock
strikes four, then two, then seven, then goes wild.
A pause. More articles come in from all sides.
Suddenly they all break into pieces.

Silence.)

THE GIRL WHO HAD EVERYTHING

Characters
FATHER
MOTHER
DAUGHTER

(The dining room. The PARENTS are sitting facing
each other at the table which is set for dinner.
FATHER and MOTHER are smiling at each other.)

MOTHER. (To DAUGHTER, off stage) Are you ready,
dear?

DAUGHTER. (Off stage, impatiently) In a minute.

MOTHER. All right. (She smiles at FATHER, who smiles
back at her.

DAUGHTER enters grandly showing off her dress.)

DAUGHTER. Well, what do you think?

(PARENTS nod delightedly. DAUGHTER looks down
at her dress.)

I'm not sure, I think I liked it better when I bought it.

FATHER. Eh?!

MOTHER. No, no... yes! ... er... do you want some
dinner?

DAUGHTER. Dinner?

MOTHER. Yes, dear.

DAUGHTER. Yes. (She goes over to table; on her way she turns the radio on and off and flicks through some magazines.) No. I... I... don't know.

MOTHER. But sweetheart...

DAUGHTER. (Violently) I've changed my mind! Haven't I got the right to change my mind?

FATHER. Of course, dear, of course.

DAUGHTER. (Calming down) Yes.

(She goes to the table, stands near it. A pause. Suddenly she sits.)

MOTHER. Shall I get your dinner?

(DAUGHTER looks at her, smiles then starts laughing. FATHER and MOTHER join in.

MOTHER goes out to kitchen.

DAUGHTER takes a cigarette and lights it.)

FATHER. I didn't know you smoked. When did you start?

DAUGHTER. Just now. (Putting the cigarette out.) Now I've given up.

FATHER. I see...

(DAUGHTER gets up, walks around the room.)

Good day at the office?

DAUGHTER. I've left.

FATHER. Eh?... Oh... I see... yes! (Giggles.) What happened?

DAUGHTER. Nothing.

FATHER. Oh! I see... (Laughs.)

> (MOTHER enters, still smiling, holding a tray. Seeing FATHER laughing she merrily joins in and merrily puts the tray down on the table.)

DAUGHTER. Soup!

MOTHER. Soup...

DAUGHTER. I don't want any soup.

FATHER. (To MOTHER, delightedly) She doesn't want any soup!

MOTHER. Oh! Perhaps you'd like something else then?

DAUGHTER. (Thinking it over) Ice cream.

MOTHER. Ice cream?... Oh... Ice cream!

> (MOTHER exits to kitchen)

FATHER. Well, what are you going to do now?

DAUGHTER. Drive lorries.

FATHER. Eh?... Really...

DAUGHTER. (Changing her mind) ... Err...

FATHER. That's great!

> (MOTHER enters with tray - still smiling.)

MOTHER. Here you are dear.

FATHER. (Excitedly to MOTHER) You'll never guess...

DAUGHTER. I don't want to eat.

> (A pause.)

FATHER. So you're going to be a lorry driver!

70

MOTHER. How exciting!

DAUGHTER. (Sharply) No! A dustman.

FATHER & MOTHER. (Momentarily lost) Eh?...
    (Delightedly again) Ooooh... Yoohoo.

DAUGHTER. (Pointing at the food) On the chair.

MOTHER. What?

DAUGHTER. (Firmly) Put the food on the chair.

> (MOTHER puts plate on chair. DAUGHTER sits on the
> table and bends down towards the plate. She cannot
> reach it, so she now lies on top of the table and
> manages to eat from the plate. The PARENTS smile
> approvingly. She leans forward and then bends down to
> look underneath the table.)

> How long has all this furniture been here? You ought
> to get rid of it. I'll start with the rubbish in my room
> now! (She gets down from the table.) No! I'll get out
> myself. I'll get a room. No. I'll go to a hotel. I've
> stayed here too long. Yes. (She puts on her coat.)

FATHER. Where are you going?

DAUGHTER. I need a holiday.

> (DAUGHTER exits.

> PARENTS smile happily at each other. MOTHER clears
> table and exits to kitchen. FATHER picks up a paper
> and starts reading. MOTHER returns.

> DAUGHTER appears at the window)

DAUGHTER. Yoohoo!

> (FATHER and MOTHER start.)

FATHER. (Seeing DAUGHTER) Ohhh...

MOTHER. (Smilingly, waving to DAUGHTER) Yoohoo!

(FATHER joins her.)

DAUGHTER. Look! (She stands up and stretches her hands.)

FATHER. Had a good holiday?

DAUGHTER. (Stretches a leg outwards) Look! Like a
tightrope walker.

(She loses her balance for a moment but regains it.
FATHER and MOTHER laugh and applaud her.)

FATHER. Well... coming in?

DAUGHTER. You want me to come in? Very well, here I
come. (She points to the room then down to the street.)
In here or down there? (She jumps into the room.)
Good evening.

FATHER. Good afternoon.

DAUGHTER. It depends on your point of view, doesn't it?
I got a new job today. I'm going to be a news photo-
grapher. (Moves to bedroom door and stands there
self-mockingly) You know, freezing life on sheets of
paper.

MOTHER. Marvellous.

FATHER. And she climbed all the way up, isn't she clever?

(Both PARENTS start laughing delightedly. The laughter
grows wilder until it becomes hysterical. DAUGHTER
looks at them. She tries to say something but they go
on laughing. She tries again and again but they don't stop.
She gives up and exits.

PARENTS freeze with laughter on their faces.

Lights change. PARENTS resume their seats at the
table as at the beginning of the scene. FATHER and
MOTHER are looking at each other more and more

impatiently. Slowly they begin to mumble.)

MOTHER. (To DAUGHTER off stage, aggressively) Are you coming?

DAUGHTER. (Off stage, pleasantly) Just a sec!

MOTHER. (To FATHER) She's never ready!

FATHER. I don't know what she does in there.

(DAUGHTER enters. PARENTS mumble.)

DAUGHTER. Sorry. (Pointing to her dress) Do you like it?

MOTHER. Aren't you going to sit down?

DAUGHTER. (Going to table) I'm not late.

(MOTHER, ignoring her, goes out to kitchen. FATHER grudgingly agrees. DAUGHTER sits. FATHER mumbles.

MOTHER returns with tray. They eat in silence. Finish the meal. FATHER looks at the DAUGHTER.)

FATHER. (To DAUGHTER) That's a new dress, isn't it?

DAUGHTER. Yes.

(A pause. FATHER begins reading the paper. MOTHER begins to clear the table and takes the tray back to the kitchen. Both mumbling all the time.)

FATHER. How's the job?

DAUGHTER. (Indifferently) Ohhh... O.K.

FATHER. What do you mean O.K.?

DAUGHTER. Oh... well, you know...

FATHER. The trouble with you is that you can't be bothered with anything, can you?

DAUGHTER. It's not that, Father...

FATHER. What is it then?

(MOTHER enters.)

DAUGHTER. Well, I mean... It's not as if...

MOTHER. They're all the same. Just look at her. They have every opportunity and what do they do with it?

DAUGHTER. Oh, please...

FATHER. It's time you got some sense. With your intelligence, I just can't understand why you don't make something of yourself.

DAUGHTER. I don't know... I'm not that sort of person.

MOTHER. What sort of a person are you?

(DAUGHTER shrugs. Gets up.)

MOTHER. And I suppose you're going out again tonight.

(DAUGHTER walks to her bedroom door.)

And don't be late!

(DAUGHTER hesitates for a moment by the door and turns back as if she had decided to say something. She seems unable to find the right words. She struggles, then gives up and exits.

Lights change. PARENTS resume their seats at the table as at the beginning of the scene. FATHER and MOTHER are looking at each other with expressions of utter boredom.)

DAUGHTER. (On entering) Dinner ready?

(PARENTS get up and put on their coats.)

MOTHER. It's in the oven dear, help yourself. We're

going out.

DAUGHTER. O.K.

(She sits down and remains motionless until the end of this part of the scene.)

FATHER. Now look here love, don't get upset.

DAUGHTER. I'm not.

FATHER. We do understand you dear, but you know, you must...

DAUGHTER. I know.

MOTHER. You know we do all we can for you.

DAUGHTER. Yes.

FATHER. (Sits down beside her) Now look dear, we've never tried to impose ourselves on you.

DAUGHTER. No...

FATHER. We've never tried to interfere with what you wanted, and we never forced you to do anything.

DAUGHTER. It's not...

FATHER. Did we?

DAUGHTER. No.

FATHER. And I think I can say you could always come to me or to Mother like a friend, and freely and openly discuss your problems with us.

DAUGHTER. Yes, I know. I'm very grateful. I... I really think you're marvellous, both of you.

MOTHER. Now then if you've got a problem we'll talk about it.

DAUGHTER. I haven't got a problem.

MOTHER. Of course you haven't.

FATHER. You never did, did you?

DAUGHTER. No...

MOTHER. Now if there was something...

DAUGHTER. It's not that...

FATHER. What do you mean?

DAUGHTER. That's got nothing to do with it.

MOTHER. So what is it?

DAUGHTER. (With great effort) It's... It's...

FATHER. Come on, tell us...

DAUGHTER. It's...

(She stops, calms down, goes towards her bedroom
door, turns back, smiles. The PARENTS smile back,
she starts laughing violently. PARENTS smile, fade.
They exit by the street door. Her violent laughter
suddenly freezes on her face.

Lights change. PARENTS enter without their coats
and resume their seats at the table as at the beginning
of the scene. DAUGHTER looks at them. A pause.
Then she speaks slowly and quietly)

DAUGHTER. In the beginning there was a home, a father,
a mother... (Stops - starts again) In the beginning...
(Stops) One day, one moment, in one second everything
happened. No! No! In order, facts only. Kindergarten,
primary school, grammar school, university, work...
jobs... jobs... No! (She stops, tries again) Just the
facts. School friends, boys, sex - later, that is, even
before... my sex... the others... (She smiles, stops
abruptly) yours... and all these years she was

preparing herself... yes, I was... preparing...
myself for... (She stops then tries to start once
more) I... I... used to have a nightmare. I'd be in
a rocket pushing upwards... up and up and up... and
then suddenly I'd come to a stop... But then I move
on... on and on... and then I stop again... but again I
move on... and again... till I stop... and I move on
again and again I stop, and I move again and I stop
again, and I move on... and on... and on...

(She stops. A short pause. MOTHER starts crying
quietly.)

Now this is the beginning and the middle and the end...
(Pause) In the beginning there was everything... And
I was there... In the middle... here... I am here...

(Pause.)

FATHER. (Very quiet) I... don't understand... I...

DAUGHTER. (Continuing without paying any attention to
either of her PARENTS) And everything is constantly
moving and changing and shifting, forming itself everywhere, joining together, separating, reforming...
There's a horizon beyond every horizon, circle inside
each circle... everywhere, in everything.

FATHER. What's... happened to you?

DAUGHTER. Everything is flowing away from itself... I
... myself... away, away... from everything... every
minute... now this minute, this instant... like this...
everything... again... and again... (She stops, then
with great effort) One, two, three, four, five, six,
seven, eight... ten. I lost it again. In a split second.
Between one... (A pause of exactly a second) beat of
my heart and (Same pause) another, I always lose.
Time, things, possibilities, myself. Everything is too
far away... out of reach... There is nothing to cling
to... (She stops)

MOTHER. (Crying softly) You always had all you wanted...

DAUGHTER. (Goes over to MOTHER and FATHER, stretches out her hand, touches one of them) Mummy... (She touches the other) Daddy...

FATHER. (Softly) You had everything...

DAUGHTER. Me. I. Myself... There are... there are... inside me... there are (Suddenly) Listen! Listen! Someone is playing a violin in my head, a drum in my heart, a flute in my belly. Do you know what it sounds like when they are all playing together? All these... thoughts, and... feelings, and... sensations. How can I grasp them. They... just... keep moving on through me... everything around me... through me...

FATHER. What's wrong with you?

(DAUGHTER goes over to PARENTS, says nothing. Then she touches FATHER, then MOTHER, stands between them, looks at each of them, smiles then breaks away. Turns to them. A pause, then)

DAUGHTER. Have you noticed how green dissolves into blue, into red, red into black into white, white into... Staring at my wall, in my room at night, I can see the stone behind the wallpaper... (She closes and opens her eyes) I can see all the things around me. I repeat their names to myself, chair, table, hand... I use them... and... and... at the same time... all this time... no! It's not fear... not despair... not... need ... for me it's not hope or... will... that I... no! Something else... something... else... (With effort) It's so hard to... even... to... think... of... it... It's... not... a feeling... not a sensation... How shall I... How I... all of me... and more than me... How? How? How?

(She stops and controls herself. Short pause. She turns to PARENTS. She is very calm and gentle now)

Don't worry, it's not you; you did your best for me. Everyone did their best for me. Oh, no. It's not anyone or anything... or rather... it's everything, you see it's this question... the question... (With effort) Why is

there everything when there could be just nothing?
(She stops for a brief second and smiles) So, one
morning, one fine day I woke up. I was in my bed.
Above me was the ceiling, around me my room.
Everything was as usual, but suddenly I didn't know
whether to get up or not... (A pause. Very simple)
Now every morning when I wake up I know it is a
miracle and at the same time I don't understand why...

(A pause. She smiles, then laughs openly and freely.
Lights fade.)

THE EGG

or

WHICH CAME FIRST

Characters
FATHER
MOTHER
SON

(The living room. In the centre of the room stands an
immense 'egg' approximately nine feet high. There is
nobody in the room. A radio announcer's voice is heard
saying '... and that is the end of the news...' and is
immediately followed by a loud 'click' as the radio is
switched off.

SON comes in. He is very excited.)

SON. Not one word! (He stops, turns to the egg, looks at
it with great concentration.

FATHER comes in from the front door. He is carrying
a pile of newspapers, which he has a quick look through.)

FATHER. (To SON) There's nothing in the papers.

SON. Oh well, never mind.

FATHER. (Sits down going over the papers) With all the
fuss those reporters made I would have thought it'd be
all over the front pages.

(MOTHER enters from kitchen.)

MOTHER. Ready for dinner?

FATHER. (Finding something in small print on a middle page) Here's something! (Reads aloud) 'Mystery object discovery. A large, strange, egg-shaped object was found yesterday. Although its exact nature is not yet clear, a police official assured our correspondent that it was quite harmless...

(He hands the paper to SON who takes it without enthusiasm and reads the article. MOTHER joins him while FATHER goes over the other papers.)

FATHER. Oh! Here's a picture of you and the - thing.

(SON goes over to him immediately and takes the paper, reads it quickly.)

What does it say, son?

SON. Oh, nonsense...

(MOTHER takes the paper from him and reads aloud)

MOTHER. 'The unusual nature of the discovery has already aroused considerable interest in scientific circles. The Institute for Advanced Research is known to be keen to conduct a thorough investigation. Some experts, however, remain sceptical, while others diagnose it outright as a students' stunt. '

(She gives the paper back to SON. Both PARENTS look at him, then all three look at the 'egg'... A pause.)

FATHER. What is it?

SON. Hmm...

(A pause.)

FATHER. A fossil?...

SON. Er...

MOTHER. I suppose it's... er... all right?

SON. Oh yes, I'm sure it is. (He goes over to the 'egg', touches it.) Hmm... it's cold.

(A pause.)

FATHER. Well, what are you going to do with it?

SON. (With determination) I'll investigate it. I'll find out all about it.

MOTHER. But... how would you know how to investigate it?

SON. I'll learn.

(A short pause.)

FATHER. Well, it's all right with me. If you want to investigate it yourself, why not!

SON. (Getting more and more excited) I've already got some books: Archeology, Biology, Zoology!

(FATHER and MOTHER exchange slightly anxious glances.)

FATHER. Hmm... How long do you think it will take you to find out about it?

SON. I don't know (With excitement and determination) ... but I'm going to start right now. I'm sending in my notice first thing tomorrow...

MOTHER. (To FATHER) Perhaps he shouldn't...

FATHER. No... (MOTHER and SON look at him) Why shouldn't he? This could be a really big opportunity for him. We should give him all the help we can.

SON. Oh thank you, Father, thank you! Thank you Mother! (Turns to the 'egg') Just look at it! Just look at it!

FATHER. We must celebrate! We must celebrate!

(He takes out a bottle and glasses, pours some brandy,
all take a glass)

FATHER. To your discovery! To your investigations! To
your success!

ALL. To success!

MOTHER. (Tears in her eyes) Do you want some dinner,
son?

SON. Thanks Mother, I'm not hungry. I can't wait to start
work.

MOTHER. But you must eat something.

FATHER. It's all right, Mother, he's too excited... Come
on...

MOTHER. Don't work too late, sweetheart.

SON. Don't worry Mother... and...

MOTHER. It's nothing, son, it's nothing. Just as long as
you... (She kisses him.

FATHER and MOTHER exit.

SON takes off his jacket. Puts on a cardigan, takes a
book, looks for a moment at the 'egg' and then sits down
and starts to read.

The light from the window dims then changes to daylight.
He's reading, taking notes occasionally.

Enter FATHER.)

FATHER. Hello, genius! Here're the books you wanted.

SON. Oh, thank you.

FATHER. How are you getting on?

SON. Fine, fine, look at this. (He takes out a diagram)

It's a day by day report of every change.

FATHER. (Studies it) There don't seem to be many changes, do there?

SON. (Pins the diagram on the wall) I'm now working on chemistry and bio-physics. I've ordered special equipment. I hope it won't be too expensive.

FATHER. (After slight hesitation) Son... will it be much longer?

SON. What?

FATHER. Well... your investigations.

SON. Oh, don't worry, not too long.

FATHER. Another year or two?

SON. (Hesitates) I... think so.

(MOTHER enters.)

MOTHER. There's a parcel for you, son.

(SON goes over to it immediately and unwraps it. It's some sort of scientific equipment. PARENTS look at him.)

FATHER. (Gets up) Well, I think I'll go to bed.

(Short pause.)

SON. You look tired, Dad.

FATHER. Oh, it's not too bad.

SON. You work too hard.

FATHER. It's nothing, son. The main thing is that you...

SON. Everything will be fine, Father, you'll see. I'll make it up to you. I really will.

FATHER. I know, son, I know. I'll see about that new equipment. Any letters you want posted in the morning?

SON. (After a short pause in which he looks at FATHER) Eh?... Yes. Here.

FATHER. (Looks at SON. After a short pause.) Well, goodnight. Don't push yourself too hard, eh!

SON. O. K. Dad... and er...

FATHER. Keep at it, son. It will be all right.

(Exit PARENTS. SON returns to work.

Lights change. Enter MOTHER. She holds some books.)

MOTHER. More books.

SON. (Wile working) Put them down somewhere. (Goes on reading) 'The completeness and teleology of biological structure cannot be explained by the processes of the individual atoms, classified by the discovery of quantum energy.'

(FATHER enters with a parcel and books. He puts them down. SON goes over to them and unwraps the parcel. It is some other equipment. A pause.)

FATHER. Son, I want to talk to you.

SON. Eh?...

FATHER. Have you any idea how long it's been?

SON. Er...

FATHER. Five years!

SON. Hmm... It... won't be much longer. (He goes back to his work.) It's the question of the right question... a question of discipline, perhaps a question of perseverence...

FATHER. Son!

SON. What?

FATHER. Listen to me...

>(SON nods.)

>You know I've always done everything in my power to help you...

SON. (He is really preoccupied in his work) Yes, Father, thank you...

FATHER. But... I don't know... the whole thing seems wrong.

SON. What?... Yes, I'm exploring new fields. I've lots of new ideas... (He starts writing quickly.

>FATHER and MOTHER exchange looks, worried.)

SON. (Writes) Dear Professor, I was very happy to read that your opinion in this matter is similar to mine. On the other hand... (Stops writing) On the other hand... (Grabs a book, reads) 'All the... which are necessary are fused together at the same moment in the right place.' (Stops reading.)

MOTHER. Perhaps you should go out a little.

SON. (To MOTHER) What?... no, no... (Back to himself) Hmm... This means... That's contradictory, but still it's very precise... we are progressing... there's no doubt about it. (He takes another book, changes his mind, writes quickly) Dr Watson, Dr Krick, Professor Bohr.

>(FATHER sighs, gets up slowly and exits with MOTHER. SON goes on working, mumbling unintelligibly. Only now and then we can hear him muttering)

>What is it?... What is it?...

(Slowly his mumbling and muttering changes to an imitation of all sorts of mechanical noises.)

Tick-tock, clunk, clunk, clunk, poof...

(He moves about. The sounds change into words again.)

Examination, Classification, Exemplification, Qualification... What am I doing? (He turns to the books, equipment etc.) NO! NO! It's all wrong! This isn't the way. (He starts tearing and destroying the books, notes and equipment and throws them about while shouting) It's all wrong! It's all wrong!

(MOTHER enters holding some books and a picture. She watches SON for a while and then puts down the books and silently starts clearing up after him. After destroying most of the scientific stuff, he calms down and sits. With quiet determination)

Science has failed me.

(MOTHER goes over to him and hands him the picture. It's FATHER's picture in a black frame.)

MOTHER. Here, you can have this.

(SON takes the picture, looks at it and starts laughing.)

SON. (Recites)   'There once was a brainy baboon
                   Who always breathed down a bassoon
                   For he said 'It appears
                   That in billions of years
                   I shall certainly hit on a tune.''

(He laughs)

MOTHER. I'll clear up.

(She does so. SON stops laughing, looks at her, then talks to her while she goes on with her action.)

SON. We must find a different way. I shouldn't have searched from the outside. I must get inside... I must find a different question... yes! I must ask the central, the essential, the necessary question.

(MOTHER finishes her clearing up and looks at him.)

MOTHER. Shall I cook you something?

(SON looks at her but does not answer. A pause. Softly)

This... this... 'egg' has driven you mad...

(A pause. He looks at her. MOTHER exits.

Lights change. The room looks like an artist's studio. Though SON is about 40 he looks much older, his face grey and wrinkled, his dress has deteriorated, but there is still stubborness in his way of speech. He sits in the middle of the room and stares ahead. A pause.)

SON. I once read a phrase which said everything, or almost everything or rather what it had to say. Later I understood that I was wrong. The dizziness I felt was as natural as the clarity which I had felt before, or after... and just as agreeable... Sitting in my room at night, I have tried to understand the meaning of the words which floated aimlessly in my head. I have collected them together and then reduced them into words again. Then I used the words in the past tesne, present and future tenses, sometimes with a question mark, sometimes in inverted commas, sometimes even in brackets. But whenever I wrote these words down I would never make a sentence... occasionally a phrase... but never a sentence...

(A pause.)

A nervous doubt slowly crept from my belly, lower from my groin...

(He stops, smiles, starts reciting)

'Men and lions, eagles and partridges, geese, spiders' (He laughs)'I'm coming more and more to the conclusion

that a man must write without thinking of form at all'
(He laughs) What a sense of humour... wait,
(Recites)   A was an apple pie;
                B bit it;
                C cut it;
No, I've got a better one. (Recites)
                'Hickory dickory dock
                The mouse ran up the clock
                The clock struck one
                The mouse ran down
                Hickory dickory dock!'
They say that Kant spent his old age watching little
girls from his window and masturbating as much as
he could...

(He laughs faintly. A pause. He shouts)

'L'egg c'est moi!'

(A pause)

No god ever whispered anything in my ear... Not a
bird! Not even a flea!

(MOTHER comes in holding a picture, in a black frame
like FATHER's. She goes over to SON and gives him
the picture.)

MOTHER. Here, you can put it next to your father's.

(MOTHER exits.

He remains with the picture in his hand, looks at it,
then puts it next to FATHER's. A pause. He turns,
looks around then methodically destroys every painting
and sculpture in the room. Then he stands facing the
thing. Quietly)

SON. What is it? (Stronger) What is it? (Gradually he
becomes more and more stubborn) I want an answer.
I want the real answer. Here, now! I've studied,
searched, investigated. I've never stopped. All my
life, all my life. Now's the time.

(He stops for a second, trying to make up his mind
what he should do next)

All right then. From now on I'll just wait. Ten, thirty
years, however long I've got. I'll wait till the answer
comes, till the solution comes. Until it comes to me...
Come to me, come to me, come to me! I want you.
(He cries out with great rage and helplessness) I want
you. (He gets very weak) Come... to me... come...
I... want an answer.

(He freezes. Lights go down. Evening. He is old, but
looks even older. From the first words he utters it is
obvious that he has lost his mental balance. Giggles
quietly while looking sideways towards the thing)

What was that? (Listens) Yes, yes it was very clear
this time. (Giggles) A voice... a... murmur... yes...
(He listens intently but does not hear anything) Hmmm,
I just need a bit more patience... (He turns to the
thing) Never mind, my little bitch, never mind, I'll
wait... I've got plenty of time.

(Suddenly he smiles to himself peculiarly and goes
towards the thing. He knocks on it with his finger.)

Hello. Anyone in? (Listens) No reply. Nobody home...

(He moves away. Suddenly he gets angry)

Fool! Idiot! Open your mouth! (Quickly regretting what
he has just said) No, no, you are no idiot, you are
clever. Come on, talk to me, I know you can talk. I
won't tell anyone. We are all alone here. Only you and
me... (He waits a moment, then angrily again) Talk!
Talk, you fool! (Suddenly) No, no! (Suddenly in a
different tone) Hello, Professor, and what have you
to say to defend your latest theories... shhh... I can
hear something... (To the thing) What do you say?
You say you love me? Oh, I love you, I love you...
(Sonorously) Do you take this woman to be your lawful
wedded wife?... But of course, of course... Do you
know my parents? They sacrificed their lives for me,
you know, for me and my... er... er... (Changing

his tone suddenly) Where is that damn book? I have to
check it electrostatically... I am hungry. (Change of
tone) Sit down children.

(He puts some broken sculpture in front of the thing)

Now eat up nicely... when you are grown up, you'll
be scientists or artists... whatever you like. (Sings)
Baa baa black sheep... etc. (Stops suddenly. To the
thing) Don't worry Dad, I'll make it up to you, you'll
see... What do you say, Mother? (Gets angry) Come
on Professor, speak up! Speak up. (Change of
attitude) My love... my wife... my daughter... my
child. Tell me what you want to tell me, don't be
afraid, I am waiting for you, only for you... sshh... I
can hear a voice! Here it comes... Music! Trumpets!
Drums! In honour of... in honour of...

(He bows in all directions and shouts)

My lords, ladies and gentlemen, most distinguished
guests, we hereby honour the discoverer of the greatest
secret in the history of mankind... sshh... I hear...
I hear something... sshh...

(He freezes, his eyes stare emptily. Lights turn to
daylight. White bright burning light. He is very old
now and ill. He is lying near the thing. Slowly he gets
up. He is very weak. He trembles and from time to
time he coughs violently. When he talks it is a great
effort. Sometimes he whispers out of weakness)

It's cold... oohh..

(He gets up, almost cannot stand. His hand slowly
caresses the shell of the thing)

Was it just weakness? Will it always be weakness?
What sort of weakness is it? Isn't such weakness strength?
Is it strength?

(He moves slowly to the thing)

This horrible feeling as if nothing has passed between

myself and all the things I've seen, that I've heard,
that I've touched... (Very weakly) all these years...
my life... Is this all it is about? All that will be left?
(He looks around shuddering out of weakness and cold)
My life...

(He touches the 'egg' and then walks to the corner)

Tell me now... you can tell me now... (He stops,
stands up and looks around again) You see my life was
full of beauty and courage and meaning... now...
(He sits down in corner) ... now...

(He dies.

A pause. The 'egg' breaks. From inside it rolls out
another, much smaller egg which, having stopped,
slowly gets bigger and bigger until it reaches the
size and shape of the original 'egg'.

A pause.)

SO?

Characters
FATHER
MOTHER
SON
DAUGHTER
GRANDMOTHER
A MAN
A WOMAN

(The living room. Curtain rises. The room is empty.
For thirty seconds nothing happens.

Enter FATHER and SON in pyjamas.)

FATHER. Mor... mor...

SON. Like clockwork.

(A clock strikes. They go out togther.

Enter MOTHER and DAUGHTER in nightdresses. They
giggle, exit and return immediately.)

DAUGHTER. Co... co... ffee.

(MOTHER giggles. They exit.

Enter FATHER.)

FATHER. Morning.

(MOTHER and DAUGHTER enter, giggle and exit.

FATHER exits.

Enter GRANDMOTHER in a wheelchair.)

GRANDMOTHER. What a morning.

(Lights change to evening.)

What an evening.

(Lights change to day.

FATHER enters dressed in a dinner jacket. He bows to GRANDMOTHER and sits in a chair. In his hands, a model of a guillotine.)

FATHER. Some millions, thousands, hundreds, tens, ones in the Thirty Years War... one by one, one by one... (He releases the blade of the guillotine - 'click'.

Quick blackout. Soft music from a loudspeaker. The voice of a pop singer. A spot on GRANDMOTHER.)

GRANDMOTHER. Cuckoo!

(Quick blackout. A voice over the loudspeaker with a heavy American accent - 'Stick 'em up! Nobody move! You're covered!'

Full light on stage. Enter FATHER and MOTHER in everyday clothes.)

FATHER. Do you know how long I've been living in this country?

MOTHER. Who wants to know?

FATHER. Yes, who?

MOTHER. I do.

FATHER. All I care about is my home, my family...

MOTHER. And the children.

FATHER. That's obvious, don't interrupt. We must
protect ourselves, protect one another. We are a
united family and that means that we are...

MOTHER. A community.

FATHER. Exactly. Didn't I tell you not to interfere? Well,
more that we are...

MOTHER. A people.

FATHER. You have to interfere, don't you? Just as I'm
getting some satisfaction from what I'm saying...
What was I saying?...

MOTHER. A world.

FATHER. Stop taking the words out of my mouth!

(MOTHER looks at him. They wait looking at each other.)

MOTHER. You've got one more word.

FATHER. I know

MOTHER. So why don't you use it?

FATHER. I don't feel like it?

MOTHER. Coward.

(FATHER laughs)

All right, I can wait.

(They both get up and stand facing each other like
wrestlers. They mime wrestling.)

MOTHER. (Getting the advantage) A universe!

(FATHER falls clutching his balls. MOTHER puts on
a black head scarf)

FATHER. (Getting up) Very funny, very funny. We'll see

who's faster next time.

MOTHER. (Change of tone - very kindly) What about the children?

FATHER. (Becoming kindly) Oh yes, our children.

(CHILDREN enter. SON is wearing a clown's costume. DAUGHTER is dressed as a nun.)

SON & DAUGHTER. (Chanting)
'A' is for apple, rosy and red,
'B' is for baby, who's going to bed,
'C' is for...

DAUGHTER. Our parents don't understand us.

SON. No they don't.

(PARENTS leave the room.

GRANDMOTHER hiccoughs.)

DAUGHTER. Look! A grandmother.

SON. Another curiosity.

(SON takes off his costume, remains in his under-clothes. So does DAUGHTER.)

DAUGHTER. You are beautiful.

SON. So are you.

(GRANDMOTHER yawns.
They dress in everyday clothes.
GRANDMOTHER yawns.)

Look at that mouth.

DAUGHTER. What about our Father and Mother?

(Blackout. Voice over loudspeaker - 'Ladies and gentlemen, tea break.' Pop music. The voice again.

'Put a lion in your tummy.' Roar of a lion. Music
continues, PARENTS enter.

Lights up. Music stops. FATHER is dressed in an old
fashioned swimming costume, MOTHER in 17th century
costume.)

DAUGHTER. (To SON) Look at them!

FATHER. Sorry.

(FATHER and MOTHER change their costumes to
everyday clothes.

Voice over loudspeaker - 'End of tea break.' Another
voice - 'Please resume your seats.' Another voice -
'The flight for Bermuda leaves in 30 seconds.'

GRANDMOTHER begins to whistle.)

FATHER. (To GRANDMOTHER) Stop it.

(She continues to whistle. To MOTHER)

Tell her to stop it.

(MOTHER exits)

SON. (Referring to GRANDMOTHER) She's at it again.

GRANDMOTHER. If you only knew what a man your
Grandfather was.

FATHER. We know.

GRANDMOTHER. He could lift a table with his teeth.

FATHER. We know.

GRANDMOTHER. He could bend iron with...

FATHER. We know.

GRANDMOTHER. He was...

FATHER. (Shouts) Enough!

(GRANDMOTHER whistles.

MOTHER enters, her belly swollen. She knits.)

FATHER. What do you think you are doing?

MOTHER. Can't you see? I'm knitting.

FATHER. I see, I see. What have you done to yourself?

MOTHER. What do you mean?

FATHER You know bloody well what I mean, damn you!

MOTHER. I don't even know what you are talking about.

FATHER. Take it out.

MOTHER. What?

FATHER. Take it out I tell you.

MOTHER. Leave me alone.

FATHER. (Getting more and more hysterical) Take it out, you hear me? Take it out!

MOTHER. No! No!

(FATHER goes over to her and takes out from under her clothes the rags she has there.)

FATHER. (While taking out the rags) You shouldn't do it to me, you hear. You shouldn't do it. Take it out. Take it out. (He throws the rags on the floor and stamps on them.)

MOTHER. (Cries) You promised.

FATHER. If you do it once more, by God I'll kill you!

MOTHER. (Crying) You lied to me! You cheated. Liar!

98

Liar!

(GRANDMOTHER whistles to herself, peacefully. A pause. Suddenly a window opens.)

FATHER. Who opened the window?

(No one reacts.)

Close it!

(SON goes over to window, closes it, returns to his place. Pause.)

SON. What are we waiting for?

(The window opens again.)

FATHER. Who opened that window again?

(No reaction.)

Will someone close it properly?

GRANDMOTHER. Air! Air!

(SON closes window again. The opposite window opens. They all look at it. A pause. DAUGHTER closes it.)

FATHER. That's what you all want, to get away from here.

DAUGHTER. To go where?

FATHER. What's wrong with it here?

GRANDMOTHER. If only Grandfather was alive...

MOTHER. What's it like out there? (Opens first window)

DAUGHTER. Is it summer?

MOTHER. It's raining and the trees, the grass, the roof-tops, people's heads are all covered with little white pearls.

FATHER. Close the window. There is a draught.

GRANDMOTHER. Air... air...

MOTHER. What a way to live. (Closes window.)

FATHER. That's my line.

MOTHER. It's the same everywhere.

SON. But the land...

FATHER. That's already a political question.

DAUGHTER. The sea?

FATHER. (Angry) The State is us.

SON. Wrong. We are the State.

FATHER. All right, after you.

SON. Excuse me, you first.

GRANDMOTHER. Grandfather was the first.

SON. Yeah, and look where he is now.

GRANDMOTHER. You think you are so much better, eh

FATHER. All right! All right! Get to work.

> (GRANDMOTHER whistles. To GRANDMOTHER)

> You too, old bag!

> (They all begin to whistle and bring in weapons,
> ammunition, flags etc. Then they barricade all
> entrances to the room.)

> That's it. Now this is home.

> (Sounds of shooting from outside. GRANDMOTHER
> starts to whistle again. Sounds of more shooting, a

FATHER. Somebody has got in.

SON. Who is it?

DAUGHTER. How?

MOTHER. When?

DAUGHTER. Are you sure?

FATHER. Someone is in here I tell you.

SON. How did they get in?

DAUGHTER. They?

MOTHER. (Frightened) What?

FATHER. What the hell do you want?

MOTHER. Who are they?

SON. We ought to find out.

DAUGHTER. Are they saying anything?

MOTHER. What are they doing?

FATHER. How did they get in here in the first place?

SON. They ought to be taken out.

FATHER. Right.

DAUGHTER. Shall we talk to them?

FATHER. Rubbish.

ALL. What?

FATHER. There is nobody there.

ALL. (Great relief) Thank God.

(Short pause.)

GRANDMOTHER. Here they are.

(A pause.)

FATHER. Were they here all the time?

SON. (To FATHER) Talk to them.

FATHER. Are you mad?

DAUGHTER. We must do something.

MOTHER. What?

DAUGHTER. I don't know but we must, we can't go on
living like this.

FATHER. Yes, it's a matter of the utmost importance to
us all.

(A pause.)

ALL. So what are we going to do? What? What?

FATHER. Rubbish.

(FATHER takes out a machine-gun and shoots the two
MEN. They fall.)

SON. That's it. It was a matter of life and death for them.

THE MAN. (Lifts himself and with his last breath) We...

FATHER. (Bending low to hear him. The MAN whispers
something and falls. FATHER straightens up) I think
he said they were from the Electricity Board.

(Black out. Lights in fast.)

Damned technology. All I care about is my home, my
family, my children, my country and (Looks at
MOTHER. She tries to speak but he is too fast for her

104

...is time.) the universe!

MOTHER almost faints. He gives a satisfied laugh.

...ouse lights come up and there is a drum roll (long)
...uring which the two characters on the floor get up,
...nd, taking off their cloaks and masks, reveal them-
...elves as the QUEEN and PRINCE PHILIP.

...shock of recognition from the family who shuffle
...to a line along the front of the stage, with their
...acks to the audience as if to be presented to their
...ajesties.

...he drum roll ends and the National Anthem begins.
...reeze. After the first few bars it fades and continues
...uietly until the end of the play. The freeze breaks.

...he QUEEN and PRINCE PHILIP do the final honours,
...o up to and individually shake hands with the members
...f the cast.)

...N. (To FATHER) Well done, thank you all.

...IP. (Mumbling and repeating the above) ...

...N. (To MOTHER) Very amusing.

...PHILIP same)

...N. (To SON) We found it highly stimulating.

...PHILIP same)

...N. (To DAUGHTER) You were terribly good.

...PHILIP same)

...N. (To GRANDMOTHER) Errr...

...PHILIP same.

...After this slight hesitation the QUEEN exits upstage
...ollowed, as always, at a respectable distance, by

105

PHILIP. The QUEEN and PRINCE PHILIP may be replaced by the heads of state appropriate to the country where the play is performed.

The curtain comes down quickly so that it cuts the cast off from the rest of the stage. They get back as best they can.)

C AND B PLAYSCRIPTS

		Cloth	Paper
PS 30	THE LUNATIC, THE SECRET SPORTSMAN AND THE WOMEN NEXT DOOR and VIBRATIONS by Stanley Eveling	25s	9s
* PS 31	STRINDBERG by Colin Wilson	25s	9s
* PS 32	THE FOUR YOUNG GIRLS by Pablo Picasso trans. Sir Roland Penrose	25s	9s
PS 33	MACRUNE'S GUEVARA by John Spurling	25s	9s

* All plays marked thus are represented for dramatic presentation by:
C and B (Theatre) Ltd, 18 Brewer Street, London W1